The Superior Educator

A Calm and Assertive Approach
to Classroom Management
and Large Group Motivation

Never be powerless in the classroom again.

Unlock the secrets to calm
and assertive leadership.

Learn to manage large groups
and move them to success.

Stephen T. McClard

www.SuperiorEd.com

Contents

Concluding Thoughts

I dedicate this book to my father,

Don McClard
1931-1989

"My life has been a poor attempt to imitate the man. I'm just a living legacy to the leader of the band."

Lyric from, "The Leader of the Band" by Dan Fogelberg

Acknowledgments

I would like to thank the following people for assisting me with this book:

I would like to say thank you to Tony Boyd, Sr., for the incredible cover art. Thank you to my friend Jeff Waters for the helpful advice along the way. Thank you to Dr. Robert Gifford for taking the time to read my book and write the foreword. Additionally, thank you, Dr. Gifford, for being an amazing role model and mentor since seventh grade.

Thanks to my trophy wife for being amazing!

To Andrew and Parker, the best sons a father could ever have or hope for.

Especially, thank you to my mother and father for helping me become who I am today.

Foreword

A desire of every teacher is that many of our students will have had their lives enriched positively and that at least a few of them will have been sufficiently influenced to assimilate our teachings, while developing basic concepts even further. In this way, effective teaching practices become the culmination of generations of teachers and students.

A good teacher welcomes students who question the status quo, and Stephen McClard was just such a student. He has continued to question, explore, and develop his knowledge and techniques as a teacher and shares his journey as well as discoveries with the reader.

There is no shortage of self-help books on the market, except for teachers. This book fills this void by presenting ideas centered on the importance of examining our own behaviors, attitudes, and self-expectations as they relate to particular teaching techniques. Not only does this book contain numerous "gems of wisdom" for the novice teacher, but it will be enlightening to the experienced teacher as well.

The book is organized so that reading a chapter a week, while assimilating the techniques into your own teaching style, will provide you with many of the skills necessary to maintain better classroom management and to enhance the learning environment. Enjoy using this "field manual for survival in the classroom."

Robert M. Gifford, D.M.A.
Professor Emeritus of Music

Introduction

Are you sick of teaching through distraction? Is the routine of poor behavior in your classroom driving you to substance abuse? Do you get the feeling that nobody is listening to you and you are not receiving the respect that you deserve?

If you have been searching for a way to take control of your classroom, now you have it. Why spend your best years fighting stress and disappointment? Take charge now and learn the secrets to a better life and rewarding educational experience for you and your students.

In this book, you will enter a world where you are in charge of every situation. It does not matter whether your classroom is a large group, such as a band or choir, or just a few students. By applying a simple set of guidelines and psychological strategies, you will soon become the amazing teacher you dreamed of becoming when you started your career. As an added bonus, this book will help you prevent heart disease, control diabetes, lower your blood pressure, heighten creativity, improve your physical appearance, increase coordination, strengthen your immune system, lose weight, and add 20 years to your life.

Now that I have your attention, let me say that the claims made above are not necessarily a fantasy and can become a reality. This is entirely up to your drive, determination, and self-control as an individual. By changing one person, you can change the lives of thousands.

All teachers, no matter the leadership style, will make mistakes, upset parents, and do amazingly dumb things in the classroom. As I read over the words that I have written in this book, I realize that many of these best educational practices are, in reality, some of my own personal weaknesses.

After reading this book, you may think that I must be some kind of super-teacher who has total control over all aspects of his classroom and program. I'll be the first to admit that this is not always the case. I have had some amazing times in the classroom and have moved groups of students to wonderful successes. When this has happened, I can say with confidence that it was when I followed my heart as a teacher and tried to see the good in my students and myself. I am continually striving toward this goal—the goal of continuous personal development for my students and myself.

We all have weaknesses to address and personality problems to iron out. We all wish that we could be the people who we admire most, but there are always times that we fail to meet these ideals. We are all human, after all. No matter how much we admire others for their work, we can bet that they make mistakes just like us. The grass may not always be greener on the other side, but it will always look that way. Your job is to keep your own "lawn" looking the best you can.

Let me give you a story that will relate to this idea. One of the interesting jobs that I have done with my spare time is to take old upright pianos and convert them into computer desks. I have built these desks and sold them all over the United States. This unique hobby came from my background as a piano tuner and technician.

I was in my garage one day, looking at a uniquely crafted old upright piano that I had recently acquired. It was mahogany and had solid, hand-carved legs. The only problem was that it had a huge crack in the soundboard. That was the end of the road for this piano. I looked it over for a few minutes, then walked into my house and sat down at the computer.

My computer desk was nearly in pieces, so I looked over at my wife and said, "I'm going to take that old piano out there and make it into a desk." Needless to say, that didn't go over very well. My wife said she would not allow me to waste our money in that way. A few minutes after she said that, I was in the garage tearing it apart and starting to build my new desk.

My wife was not very happy with me for several weeks. As the desk came together, she slowly admired the new piece of furniture. The final coat of finish was on, and she was moving furniture around to make room for our new desk. She even invited family and friends over to see her new and unique piece of furniture.

A few years later, I had the opportunity to build a computer desk for a Hollywood producer. Over the next month or so, we communicated about the building of the desk and became friendly enough with each other to talk about life, including aspects of our careers and families. I saw him as a successful Los Angeles hotshot and me as a lowly teacher from the Midwest. What I discovered as I talked with him was that we were very similar individuals despite our different backgrounds.

No matter how we see others, we are all human and make pretty much the same mistakes. We share the same desire— the desire for acceptance. If you want to be a great teacher, the only real job you have is to show students that you accept and appreciate them. Beyond that, you help them see their own potential and help them reach for success.

Let's be honest. Seeing the good in everyone is difficult. Being all things to all people is impossible, making the job of a teacher or coach demanding and frustrating. At other times, being an educator can be a rewarding and life-changing experience. The journey is never one of constant success.

Numerous factors in education are beyond the reach of the classroom teacher. Despite this fact, it is possible to make a significant impact on your students' lives and experience less stress from day to day. You have the power to make this happen.

The secret of this book is in the next statement. **Enjoy the successes you have, constantly grow in your understanding, and learn from your failures.** The concepts found in this book are merely an attempt to help you achieve this simple goal.

The ideas in this book are my thoughts on classroom management and large-group leadership learned over the course of my career in education. Most of the insights here are gleaned from my own personal experiences and reflect years of trial and error. Some of the techniques that I share in this book are passed down to me through the advice of other amazing teachers such as my father. Yet other strategies are learned through the observation of other individuals outside the field of education and through my studies in psychology and philosophy. No matter the source, I consider these my best practices, worthy of sharing with other educational professionals.

I can only hope that, in some small way, this book might spur you on to effective ideas of your own. Through your journey as an educator, you will hopefully realize that you can succeed in the classroom despite the daunting obstacles that lay before you. If you get nothing else from this book, remember this truism: **If you want to succeed, then you need to hurry up and keep failing.** Success is found at the farthest edge of failure. If you do not push to the edge and look over, you will never know what you might have discovered on the other side.

Preface

"There are three ways to attain wisdom. The first is reflection, which is the highest, the second is imitation, which is the easiest and the third is experience, which is the bitterest." Confucius, 500 B.C.

This book started with Chapter 2 when I was sitting in a graduate class thinking of student misbehavior. I had my laptop open to the writings of Abraham Maslow when I keyed in on his Hierarchy of Needs. I came to the realization that many of the behaviors I was dealing with in the classroom were a result of unmet needs from the family. Many years of working around these missing needs have helped me develop a set of strong routines that have assisted in bringing success into the lives of my students.

At the end of the process, I realized that I wrote this book for myself first. Reflecting on my own weaknesses shows me just how much work I still have in front of me before I become the master teacher I envision. I have noticed through the years that the work I do to enhance my own personality and character is directly tied to the development of my students. The better I develop myself, the more my students achieve.

So, how do we arrive at this kind of success in the classroom? I have spent eighteen years in education figuring out that question, and here is what I have found: to lead the many, you must first lead the one. The "one" is you. Self-improvement as an educator is where success will start. Gaining self-confidence, self-control, and self-esteem will be your focus throughout this book. Being in control of one person will allow you to have control of thousands if that is what you want to do. Small class or large, it does not matter. You are the only "one" you can improve with certainty. From there, it is a matter of having the right tools, keeping them sharp, and keeping your optimism high.

As you consider what I said above, ask yourself these questions: What drives you in life? Why do you own the vehicle that you own? Why did you choose its color the way you did? Do you own more vehicles than you need and why? Why do you take vacations, and how did you pick where you would go? I could keep going, but the answer to all these questions is need. Everything in your life is done the way it is done because of need. Need is in the driver's seat for every step you take.

When you are hungry, you eat. When you are thirsty, you drink. When you want to enhance your self-esteem, you purchase a shiny red motorcycle and try not to crash. When you want to stroke your ego, with disregard to your pocketbook, you buy a sports car. The need for constant stimulation to our emotions and desires is found in our ongoing thirst to fill need.

Right now, you are reading this book because you have a need. You have a desire for better classroom management so you will have a satisfying career in education. To fill this need, you must first realize what you are missing. You must be missing something, or you would already be meeting your needs. What I am hoping you see from my book is that you can only solve your problems by improving one person first. That person is you.

As you read, you will notice that I have included many paraphrased quotes from the teachings of Confucius. The translations that I reference are by James Legge (1815-1897), from his *Chinese Classics* series. Despite the fact that Confucius did not pen these words himself, I attempt to stay true to the original message within my paraphrase. There are many sources that are available to give us an approximation of his philosophies and teachings, and the paraphrasing found in this book will attempt to stay as true to the original philosophy as possible.

Confucius' thoughts, originating around 500 B.C., have been a dominating influence in the cultures of China and the Near East. There are many aspects of his writings that speak to the modern educator on topics such as morality, correct social relationships, sincerity, and justice. By all considerations, Confucius was the originator of all the thoughts contained within this book and his original teachings still echo through the best educational writings of our day.

In the *Doctrine of the Mean*, Confucius speaks about the characteristics of what he calls the "superior man." He defines certain qualities and characteristics within a person that lead to excellence. Within the pages of this book, I hope to reveal what it takes to become a "superior educator."

If you want to see any measure of success with your students, you must first look in the mirror and reflect on your own weaknesses. How would you need to change to become a superior educator? Give me your ear and some of your time, and together we will try to answer this question.

1
First Things First—Develop a Vision

"Success depends upon previous preparation.
Without advanced preparation, failure is inevitable."
Confucius, 500 B.C.

Development of a clear and exciting personal vision is essential to knowing what you will expect from your students and from the team you lead. This "vision" is your mental image of every aspect of your classroom or program in one short statement.

When you are in environments where you are a team teacher, the head of your department, principal, or coach, it will be essential to get your staff clearly focused on all objectives with strictly defined leadership roles and responsibilities. By revealing your vision and developing goals for your classroom, you give everyone involved a clear understanding of who you are as a leader and what you will expect on a daily basis. You should leave no question in the minds of your students and staff of their roles in the organization. Have a clearly written vision of what your activity or class looks like and engage those around you with enthusiasm for the job at hand.

All successful business leaders will take time to reflect on where they want their company to be in the future and what goals will lead them to the desired outcome. They know that motivating their workers depends on a clearly defined vision and a consistently executed plan. A well-developed vision will arouse emotions within the organization and motivate the people you lead. Even if your students never read your vision statement, they will sense that you are a teacher with a plan by your highly organized persona.

I include my personal vision statement in a director's handbook that I present to my staff to clarify leadership roles and define goals. Below is the introductory vision statement and rationale from this document.

Vision Statement: *The band program will only be as strong as the foundation and solid leadership contained within the organization. Obviously, the foundation begins at the middle school level. A quality music education must be at the forefront to achieve maximum success. This can only be accomplished through a clear plan that is consistently executed. When a solid foundation is in place, clearly defined leadership roles are paramount to constant success.*

Rationale: *After careful review of procedures and a thorough examination of student progress over my career as an educator, I have come to several conclusions about which educational practices are most effective. Observing these best practices will maximize our combined impact in the classroom and enhance student morale in a consistent manner. Clarifications in leadership roles will allow the instrumental music staff to serve students better and will enhance each student's overall experience. Duties outlined for each director will guarantee that the chain of command is followed and that leadership roles and policies are certain and not arbitrary.*

Classroom Questions and Activities

1. Write a few paragraphs outlining your future job aspirations.
2. Develop your own vision statement for your future classroom or program.

2
Understanding the Underlying Causes of Misbehavior and Underachievement

"The ancients, wanting to demonstrate illustrious virtue throughout the kingdom, first governed well their own states. Wanting to govern well their own states, they first regulated their families. Wanting to regulate their families, they first cultivated their character. Wanting to cultivate their character, they first set right their hearts. Wanting to set right their hearts, they first sought to be sincere in their thoughts. Wanting to be sincere in their thoughts, they first increased their knowledge. Increase of knowledge was found in the examination of things. Things being examined, knowledge became complete. Their knowledge being complete, their thoughts were sincere. Their thoughts being sincere, their hearts were then made right. Their hearts being made right, their character was cultivated. Their character being cultivated, their families were regulated. Their families being regulated, their states were rightly governed. Their states being rightly governed, the whole kingdom was made peaceful and happy." Confucius 500 B.C.

Eighteen years of teaching have taught me one very clear lesson: experience and emotion drives all behavior, good or bad. Because of this, I can only control a certain percentage of circumstances based on my own experiences. These circumstances are further restricted by my abilities and emotional control as a leader. If I can somehow enhance my experiences and exert greater ability and emotional control, I can, in turn, control more of my environment.

The motivating force behind any behavior, good or bad, is found both outside my sphere of influence as a teacher and caused by my influence as a teacher. Therefore, a child's behavior is motivated by unique experiences and the influence of outside forces acting on self-interests. A child's

16   www.SuperiorEd.com

ability to cope with these outside forces may be hampered by abuse, psychological disorders, developmental defects, psychological trauma, physical challenges, or neglected needs. My influence may assist in minimizing the effects of these handicaps, but in the end, I am only one piece of the puzzle.

Despite my best efforts, being connected to a child for one hour a day will not replace the needs that are left behind at home. Good old-fashioned family values are the key ingredient to stimulate a child for success. When these needs are not met, our educational process *will* leave children behind. This is *why the No Child Left Behind Act* misses the point entirely.

When you ask yourself the question of why children are left behind in American education, you are really seeking an answer to why needs are left behind. Abraham Maslow was an American psychologist who studied how needs and development are interdependent in every person. In his 1943 paper "A Theory of Human Motivation," Maslow explores a hierarchical list of needs that are present in every human.

According to Maslow, every person has basic needs that must be met for that person to progress to higher needs and ultimately arrive at the top of his "Hierarchy of Needs." The fundamental principle of Maslow's hierarchy is that some needs take precedence over others and, therefore, must be met first. Maslow's theory brings us face to face with the ultimate cause of misbehavior in the classroom.

Think of Maslow's Hierarchy of Needs like a ladder. Each need is a rung on the ladder with each successive step being dependent on the step below for progress up the ladder. These needs are broken up into five basic steps.

Step one, the most basic needs, are biological and psychological such as air, food, water, sleep, homeostasis, and excretion. The next rung on the ladder is the need for safety, which includes security, structure, resources, morality, health, and property. These two steps in the hierarchy are the basic needs that must be met by society and the family and cannot be efficiently met by educational institutions.

After children have these two basic needs met, they can now progress to the third stage in Maslow's hierarchy, which is love and belonging. Important social networks like friends, family, teachers, coworkers, classmates, coaches, and intimate relationships is the third step. It is important to restate the fact that meeting the first two needs is necessary for the third need to be met fully. As a child progresses through early development, these three areas of need play a critical role in preparing the mind for learning and must be constantly maintained and stimulated.

At this point in Maslow's hierarchy, a child can reach the fourth step, which is esteem. Self-esteem can come from a variety of sources and includes feelings such as confidence, achievement, respect for others, and respect by others. It is only at this rung of the ladder that a child begins to go beyond his surroundings to seek knowledge. He becomes a "success seeker" instead of a "failure avoider." Well-met needs are the foundation for this to take place.

Seeking knowledge is the chief desire of all educators and can be the one missing factor in a child's development. Understanding this fact gives you a clearer picture when developing your teaching and leadership style.

Transcendence is the last step in the hierarchy and is the point at which we seek a better world for others and ourselves. If it is possible to move a student in the direction of seeking knowledge, transcendence will ultimately follow later in life. It may take years for this to happen, but your influence as an educator will be critical in the movement toward this goal.

Consider Newton's first law of motion and replace the word objects with children. Objects at rest tend to stay at rest.

Objects in motion tend to stay in motion with the same speed and in the same direction unless acted upon by an unbalanced force (another moving object). Newton also said that the tendency of an object is to resist changes in its velocity and that objects at equilibrium will not accelerate. Moving children involves pushing them in the correct direction and upsetting their equilibrium. You may be the only unbalanced force in a child's life that can create the proper educational inertia. **Realize this power and use it wisely.**

Abraham Maslow said, "If the only tool you have is a hammer, you tend to see every problem as a nail." Educational institutions should not be the only tool of choice for the "nail" of student achievement. Once we realize this, we can focus on the true problems a child faces in the classroom.

It suddenly becomes clear why education is leaving students behind. Children who are "left behind" in America are experiencing a breakdown in the first four basic needs. The answer, according to politicians, is to incorporate as many social programs into education as possible and to hold teachers and school districts accountable for failing to raise standards. Teachers, who are already bogged down in preparing students for standardized tests to meet state demands, find it impossible to juggle between being a teacher, counselor, social worker, and miracle worker. On top of the juggling act, teachers receive half of the salary that any other highly educated professional would make in the business world. This situation is not making education an attractive alternative for the "best and brightest" undergraduates who want to be successful in life and receive respect in their profession.

Education will continue to be the scapegoat for the problem of social decay until lawmakers realize that education is not the source of the problem. Poorly performing schools are merely a symptom of a larger social problem. This problem will only be addressed when we are mature enough as a nation to set and enforce boundaries with decency in the media and tackle larger social problems that plague our society. We must work tirelessly to strengthen families and aid single-parent households in providing for children.

Exposure to violence, drugs, alcohol, vulgar language, and destructive behavior in the media and on the internet must be eliminated from the view of children. If not, we will continue seeing kids meet their own needs with self-destructive behavior, causing the cycle to perpetuate. If we continue modeling poor behavior in every corner of society, there will be no end to the problems we will create for children and schools.

When considering history, we see that our nation has the most advanced and effective educational traditions in the world. Most major advances in science have come from American classrooms. Telecommunications, computers, radio, television, the light bulb, and so many other inventions have come from our ability as a nation to transfer knowledge and inspire ideas. Unfortunately, most people tend to see our educational system as nothing more than the problem for children being "left behind" in our society.

In the media, you will hear such things as, "Education is nothing more than government-funded child abuse." Arrogant, uneducated comments such as these are typical of what the public is led to believe about education today. This type of deceit is dished out to the public by such personalities who seem to be merely looking for political gain or ratings on their radio programs.

As teachers, we are bombarded daily by assaults to our professionalism in the classroom. We are told that we will be held accountable for our teaching abilities and that 100% of all school children must succeed. This impossible demand is placed on teachers, but the burden truly belongs with the family. This is not hard for the average person to understand, yet politicians and the popular media do not get the point, or worse, do not want the point brought out for fear of losing votes and advertising revenue.

There is little surprise that teachers leave the classroom at a rate of one in three each year. States will be lucky if they are able to replace the nearly one million teachers that will retire in the next five years. The "best and the brightest" will continue running away from careers in education if confidence in the field is not improved and salaries continue to stagnate. Politicians need to wake up to the truth and take the focus away from educators and educational practices when dealing with the issue of failing schools. They must get on with the business of cleaning up themselves first and then focusing attention toward society instead of the classroom.

There are no easy answers to the troubles that teachers and society face. Social decay in the United States is not going away anytime soon. Until we admit to ourselves that improving family and protecting values is the ultimate answer, education in America will continue to fail for a certain number of students who, for whatever reason, have not had their basic needs met in a meaningful way by the family unit.

There have always been shifts with the curve of success in this world, and there will always be vicissitudes with any society. In the end, we have to look within ourselves to seek the greater good. When we seek to improve society by walking away from self-serving behavior, we step one rung higher on the ladder to improving the lives of everyone around us. Without realizing and affirming Maslow's genius, we are just beating nails with the same old hammer.

If you remember one thing from what I write here, remember this: If no need is "left behind," no child will ever be "left behind." This educational plan costs nothing and enriches the lives of everyone who participates.

Classroom Questions and Activities

1. Write a few paragraphs outlining your thoughts on student discipline as it relates to needs.
2. Write a few paragraphs outlining how needs played a critical role in your family life.
3. List five fears you have about becoming an educator.
4. List the areas of education that motivated you to become an educator.

3
Types of Motivators

"If you reach for the stars and hit the moon, it's okay. You've got to shoot for something and many people don't even shoot." Confucius, 500 B.C.

I have seen six basic types of students come through my classroom. I list these six categories as types of motivators. The motivator types that I list are reminiscent of Alfred Adler and Rudolf Dreikurs's social theory. I have arranged these into a quasi-hierarchial list which starts with the goal motivator type. These motivator types follow a structure where one motivator type can spiral into the next. The further the student travels down the spiral, the more difficult that it is to bring them back up to the top level of self-motivator.

Most students typically hover around motivator types one and three but can possess qualities of any or all motivator types. Students can display different types depending on which classroom they are in at the time. Students typically fit into one motivator group or another depending on the needs that are met or not met in the family. Many of the behaviors listed can come from accepted norms within the family.

Self Motivator
The self motivator has a strong desire to please others and be respected. They strive for perfection at all times. This student exhibits repetitive positive behavior that produces lasting respect and adoration from others. This student's actions are motivational to others, and self motivators are generally well liked. They have many friends, have high self-esteem, and are seen as smart and talented. They typically gain the most in life.

Social Motivator
The social motivator constantly seeks conversation with others to build self-esteem. They miss what is most important

for the future. Typically, they lack the skills and knowledge necessary to succeed at a high level, which compounds over time through lack of focus. Despite this, they do share some random characteristics with the self-motivator and may be successful in some ways and to varying degrees.

Attention Motivator

The attention motivator has an abnormal need for attention. They display repetitive actions to make themselves the center of attention. They let their personality interfere with the class and are a distraction to others. They are typically the students who are constantly in trouble and lose respect from their peers and leaders. Their actions lower their self-esteem.

Defiant Motivator

The defiant motivator lashes out to get attention. They exhibit repetitive actions to make themselves the center of attention. When asked to stop, the students become defiant and often feel mistreated after constant negative attention is focused their direction. This type of student frequently visits the office or receives referrals. The defiant motivator never sees himself or herself at fault.

Revenge Motivator

The revenge motivator is a defiant motivator who regularly hurts others physically or psychologically through comments and behavior. These students receive no respect from others in return and are routinely picked on. They often lash out with violent acts.

Non-Motivator

The non-motivator is helpless and feels inadequate. They typically wish not to be seen and hide from responsibility. They reject the smallest of educational demands placed on them. This student almost never has classroom materials. They have low self-esteem due mostly from a lack of self-motivating actions. They will often exhibit qualities of the revenge motivator.

Now that you can clearly see the different character traits associated with these six motivator types and understand the underlying causes of these behaviors, you can begin to understand how difficult it will be for you to motivate a student to achieve at a high level. Having the correct tools, experiences, abilities, and emotional controls will be essential to your success. Leading students to become self-motivated is not easy but can be done by finding the correct tools to use. Here is a story that illustrates how this has worked for me.

During my first year in my current school district, Dee Dee was in seventh grade and played in the percussion section. She was obviously talented but very shy when it came to taking the lead. My assistant director and I could see that she would be a very valuable band member for our program.

I can remember that we were looking for ways to keep the percussion section busy while we worked on a slow piece of music that did not include the percussion section, so it was my job to take them outside on the sidewalk and teach them to play trap set. When it was time for Dee Dee to learn the rock beat pattern, I could hardly get her to try it. I practically begged her to do it with no luck. We finished the rehearsal by asking the students to go home and try it out with their legs and hands. We would come back the next week and give it another go.

The next day, we were learning to play quad toms and a cadence the assistant director had written. The cadence had a particularly funky beat on the quad part, and the kids liked to dance in their seats when they heard it. Dee Dee learned the quad part the first time she played it, and I made a huge deal about it to the other drummers. This made her the center of attention, and I continued to have her play it over and over again. The kids all joined in and yelled "Dee Dee, Dee Dee!" You could see the pride she felt by her huge smile.

We then moved back into the classroom where the other members of the band were about to finish up with rehearsal. Before they put their instruments away, we had the percussion section play the cadence. Dee Dee led with the quad part, and the other band members yelled and cheered her on.

That was the trick. I appealed to her emotions. Before long, she was playing trap set as well. Her ego jumped in, and suddenly, she had a reason to get over her shyness. I had found the trick that brought her out of the state she was stuck in of non-motivator. From that day on, I did very little to stroke her ego as I had done that day. She took the initiative from that time forward to seek out the emotional rush that she felt that day.

Over the next six years, I continued to help Dee Dee feel special anytime she played anything new. When she got into jazz band, she played trap set and piano. She also sang on several songs. Music became her passion in life and became the mechanism that improved her self-confidence.

Dee Dee came from a foster home and had amazing foster parents who eventually adopted her. They actually built a room on their house just for all her musical equipment. She eventually learned to play many different instruments and developed a drive to improve her skills as a performer.

Dee Dee had a slight bit of difficulty in her stride due to a few health problems from her childhood. When it came time for marching band, I took a lightweight set of bells and made a carrier for her so that she would be able to march in parade block with us. I even put a cup holder on it for her.

This was her first year in high school. I finished the bell set while we were in our first week of band camp. About the same time, my percussion instructor was composing a cadence in C minor for our parade routine. The bell part had repeated C's in pairs. When I noticed this, I changed the key to D minor and the song now came off as DD, DD every four measures. It did not take Dee Dee long to realize that her name was in the music. This became just another way of boosting her confidence and making her feel accepted. She could see that we were working for her, and that made her feel special. Dee Dee is now in her first year of college as a full-time music student. She has plans to be the next big Christian music artist. She is also the drummer for our church orchestra, regularly sings, and plays piano in the church praise band. She is an amazing artist and brings a smile to everyone she meets.

As you can see, using the correct tools to motivate can make all the difference. It might take you some time to figure out which tool works best, but you will eventually find one that does accomplish the goal. It only takes a slight bit of effort on your part to have a huge impact on a child's life.

Before you read on, take a moment and reflect on something. If you had to be honest and sum up your childhood, all the way through to this very day, what motivator type would fit you at each stage in your development? What circumstances were happening in your life around each of these stages? Reflect on how your own motivators guided your decisions and how they were important to your development. What would it take to change these circumstances in the lives of the children you are trying to reach?

"A superior man is modest in his speech, but exceeds in his actions" Confucius, 500 B.C.

Classroom Questions and Activities

1. Which type of motivator best described you when you were young? Did your motivator type change as you matured?
2. How did your motivator type change and what were the circumstances that contributed to this change?

4
Sharpening Your New Tools

"If the only tool you have is a hammer, you tend to see every problem as a nail." Abraham Maslow

It is amazing how the simplest arrangement of words can carry such a profound meaning into our minds. Maslow understood that you must have a multitude of specialized tools to deal with life's problems. Each problem is unique. When we key into this idea and examine our own set of tools, we can start the process of learning how to select the correct tool and use it with skill.

There is an old story that I tell all my band students at least once in the seven years that I will see them. It is about two woodsmen who placed a bet. One woodsman was very old and had been cutting down trees for many years. The other woodsman was a very strong young man with a large ego. The young woodsman didn't mind letting everyone know just how strong he was. One of the men in the camp bet the young woodsman that he could not chop down a tree faster than the old woodsman. The young woodsman, trusting in his strength, set out to put the old man to shame.

When the contest began, the young woodsman started chopping his tree at a furious pace while the old woodsman sat down nearby and started sharpening his axe. Ten minutes went by, and the young woodsman was nearly halfway through the tree when the old man began to chop. After another five minutes went by, the sound of a falling tree could be heard. Which woodsman won the bet? The one with the sharpest tool won the bet with minimal effort.

The lesson here is obvious. Use the right tool and make sure that it is sharp. Keeping your tools sharp eliminates unnecessary effort. If you can sharpen your skills as a leader, you are well on your way to mastering your classroom management.

So, how do we improve our skills? What skills are most important? As this book progresses, you will find many answers to these questions. You must realize there is no "easy button" here. Working out your leadership personality is tricky to say the least. There is an area, however, that you can start working on right now with very little difficulty.

"The resolve to win, the wish for success, the urge to reach your full potential—these are the keys that will unlock the door to personal excellence." Confucius, 500 B.C.

Developing your interpersonal skills is a very important concept for an educator. If you cannot connect with the people you work with, then your professional life will be filled with difficulties. Whether it is the school lunch staff, the principal, parents, or students, everyone is important. Developing your charisma as a leader and shaping the overall perceptions of others toward you will, in some measure, determine your overall success. I have found that the least likely person is usually the one who helps me the most along the way.

I have a wonderful custodian at our high school who is just this sort of person. He came to our building my second year in this district and was there to assist me every step of the way. Having sparkling clean floors is nice, but having a friend in the building who will pick up where I make a mistake is an incredibly handy resource.

In the time I have known him, he has run the sound for our programs, recorded our concerts, set our stage, built all the cabinets in our band room, repaired equipment, and been a guest conductor at one of our concerts. He has gone out of his way to help me and been a good shoulder to lean on in times of trouble.

This custodian will call me anytime there is a problem that has not caught my attention. He helps in ways that go way beyond the scope of the average, non-certified staff member. Having a friend like this can be vital when you are in charge of a large school program. It only takes your willingness to treat the people around you with respect and dignity. You never know what the least likely person will do to make your job a success.

Several words need to define your professional life. I will not go into detail about what they mean to your interpersonal development, but just hearing the words may make you consider aspects of your own personality. Words like appreciative, compassionate, encouraging, funny, engaging, energetic, talented, thoughtful, and likeable are just a few of the words that need to describe you as a person.

> "Each of us must consider the cultivation of the person the root of everything else." Confucius 500 B.C.

You see, when you sharpen your tools as a leader, you develop your skills as a person. Being able to overcome your own demons in life and placing others first in your thoughts becomes your defining quality. It is not enough to act as if you care. You need to be genuine to be effective. Anything else will come across as condescending. We will discuss this further in successive chapters.

> "Our expectations are dependant upon diligence. The craftsman must first sharpen his tools." Confucius, 500 B.C.

5
The Right Tool – Calm and Assertive Leadership

"The good man makes it his aim to show patience and gentleness in instructing others and not to revenge unreasonable conduct. The superior man cultivates a friendly harmony, without being weak." Confucius, 500 B.C.

It has been my experience that the right tools are found in a calm and assertive leadership style. A child's perception of you forms his understanding of your mutual relationship with him. If you are calm, assertive, and in control of yourself at all times, you will ensure that your students are the same. Your expectations for yourself will be reflected in the expectations of your students and will be their guide for every choice they make in your class or activity. There are always exceptions, but for most situations, this will be the norm.

Everyone knows or has had an effective teacher who possessed mysterious personal qualities that seem to make them stand out. You may not readily see that these qualities are not mysterious or elusive at all. These qualities and traits can be reduced to two simple words—calm and assertive. The calm and assertive attitude combined with proper leadership skills is part of what it takes to redefine you as a master teacher.

The word "calm" suggests a sense of quietness and steadiness. The word evokes feelings of peace after a storm. A calm teacher is in control of emotion. Students learn that the calm teacher can be trusted and admired. A calm teacher produces a calm student.

Being calm means controlling emotion. Emotion could be the single greatest enemy of any leader, and when emotions lead your decisions, ego comes to the forefront instead of a clearly defined vision for the organization. You have heard this cliché before: Students do not care what you know until they know that you care. Bringing your raw emotions to the front of the classroom only sets the stage for feelings of failure and loss of dignity in the student. Everything you say from that point on becomes useless.

According to Richard L. Curwin and Allen N. Mendler, the main concern of a non-motivated student is personal dignity. Their book, *Discipline with Dignity*, focuses on the fact that dignity will be protected at all costs. Failure in the classroom leads a student to misbehave, and most students would rather succeed at making the teacher feel miserable than constantly failing in the activity. Inserting your negative energy only makes the situation worse. The old adage "you attract more flies with honey than with vinegar" could not be more accurate. Remaining calm in every situation will preserve dignity and assist you in motivating the worst of students.

The other side of this leadership style is being assertive. "Assertive" is a word used to describe someone who is upfront or forward. Being assertive involves putting yourself out there in ways that your self-esteem or normal personality may not always dictate. Developing a tool like assertiveness is essential to good communication in every situation. By exerting assertiveness instead of anger or dominating control, the student will perceive you in a more genuine way.

Strong leadership demands that you maintain a calm and assertive persona at all times while constantly communicating your wishes. Failure to communicate your wishes or expectations will lead to a breakdown in discipline and ultimately frustrate your every effort. When you maintain an assertive persona, you eliminate stress and anger, not only for your students but also for yourself. A calm classroom will help you communicate your expectations in a clear manner, and assertiveness will move that message across to your students.

Being calm and assertive is essential to good leadership, but being calm and assertive is useless without other necessary leadership qualities to complement this persona. To lead properly, you must first bring your own behaviors under control. I discovered this fact to be true early in my career.

When I first began teaching, I was in the habit of staying up late into the evening. I carried this pattern over from my college days. As the first few weeks of school wore on, I noticed that I was extremely tired by the time school was out for the day. By Wednesday, I would be completely wiped, and I would fall asleep as soon as I came home. I would sleep a few hours and then stay up late into the evening again.

After a month of this pattern, I notice that Mondays became the worst day of the week for me. I would snap at my students and become angry at every turn. I would sleep more during the week, but on the weekends, I would get very little sleep and wake very late in the afternoon. As Friday would approach, I noticed that my mood would lighten and my classroom experiences seemed to improve. This was mainly because I would sleep more through the week leading up to Friday.

I only taught at this school for one semester, and I later learned why my mood was so irregular. When I moved on to the next school and married my *fiancée*, my sleep habits became routine and predictable. I was no longer staying up half the night, and my mood in the classroom became much more calm and controlled. These early years of teaching taught me the importance of bringing my own behaviors and routines under control and the impact that these behaviors and routines could have on the overall climate of my classroom.

Largely, the behaviors you exhibit in the classroom will dictate your student's behaviors. Certain actions you take in your teaching style can have a huge impact on student motivation and feelings of failure. You must understand that proper leadership routines, when followed religiously, can completely alter what a student will and will not do for you. By practicing simple calm and assertive leadership routines, you can take charge of common situations instantly and avoid the need for punishment altogether.

Classroom Questions and Activities

1. Write at least one page reflecting on the ideas found in the last two chapters of this book.
2. Describe what calm and assertive looks like for your own personality.

6
Molding Your Personality for Success

"If you can one day renovate yourself, then by all means do this each day. Yes, let there be daily renovation." Confucius 500 B.C.

Most problems you have in the classroom are directly related to your leadership style and personality. Did you hear that? It is worth saying repeatedly. *You must realize that most problems you have in the classroom are directly related to your leadership style and personality.* If you cannot change this, you are stuck with the same old problems and will continue to spin your wheels. Adapting your personality to a calm and assertive leadership style will be the key to unlocking your potential as a master teacher.

So what do we say about the child's behavior? Should the child's behavior factor into the equation of leadership style and personality? The answer is yes and no. It does factor in, but you have the ability over time to change behavior. There is no magic bullet that will cure all your discipline problems. Working on discipline is a constant part of your job.

Extreme educational situations are difficult, even for the best educators. You may find yourself thinking these suggestions may not work in your situation. Remember that one tool does not fit all problems. It takes a large tool belt.

You might ask, "What's so wrong with me that I need to mold my personality?" You can only address the answer to this question by understanding how your current personality and leadership style enhances or conflicts with the goals you have for your classroom and the basic needs of your students. As you read further, you will gain a better understanding of how this can work for you.

Whether you know it or not, your personality is an engrained habit. Habits are extremely hard to break. Understanding what a good leader does by routine will assist you in adapting your current weaknesses into strengths. To accomplish this will take much thought, reflection, and personal growth. Making good routines into habits is the goal. Being perfect in your area of knowledge is not enough. **Perfection without personality is merely content without delivery.**

There are certain habits that will be the most difficult for you to break or improve. These are the habits of the heart: optimism and pessimism. By becoming the glass half-full type of person, you can take charge of any situation. Remember that the sum total of who you are is made up of what you spend your time thinking about. If you dwell on the negative side of situations, you will always be defeated. If you deny the negative, you will increase your odds of success ten-fold. You are capable of amazing things when you believe you can succeed, so why do you still doubt?

Pause a second and consider this thought. If drugs, alcohol, or other self-destructive behaviors are present in your life, then you should consider what I said in the last paragraph. The sum total of who you are is made up of what you spend your time thinking about. These destructive behaviors are what lead your life and may be your main problem in the classroom. Growing beyond this dilemma is nearly impossible because it is the very thing that occupies your thoughts constantly. This will also be true for your students. You may not be able to control this in them, but you sure can control it in yourself.

Having optimism in the darkest times can be difficult. Since optimism is related almost directly to self-esteem, finding ways to improve your self-concept becomes the focus for improving optimism. Your level of optimism and self-concept will determine whether you are more or less depressed and will define your capability to perform above or below your potential. The worst circumstances will merely bounce off you if you have amazing optimism. If your optimism is beaten down through years of poor classroom management, you may find renewed hope within the pages of this book.

To improve self-concept is to improve achievement. This is true for you and it is true for your students. If your leadership abilities were a math equation, then by taking all the skills you have learned in your life up to this point and adding this to your personality, then the sum would equal your leadership ability. Think of optimism as taking that number to the power of your level of optimism. The equation would look like this:

(Skills + Personality) (to the power of optimism) **=Leadership Potential**

The equation for pessimism would be the opposite. Pessimism takes your leadership potential away. The equation would be:

(Skills + Personality) - Pessimism=Less Leadership Potential

Anything that you can do to improve your leadership style should be practiced. Reading books on leadership, motivation, and business success is a good starting point. Using your planning time or professional days to observe other teachers is another effective idea for improving your leadership style. Use any means necessary to sharpen your axe!

I'm reminded of a trip I took to San Diego a few years ago. My principal approached me about a free trip that was being offered by the Marine Corps to observe Marine training at Camp Pendleton. I might not have taken the trip, but it was in the middle of our state proficiency test, so the students would not be in class anyway. I agreed to the trip and spent a week in California.

While I was there, I was in downtown San Diego on our evening free time and noticed that the San Diego

Community Wind Ensemble was performing a few blocks away. I took a taxi to the park and bought a ticket to the concert. I noticed from the program that the Navy Band Southwest director was going to be the guest conductor for one number.

After the concert, I went to the front of the stage and spoke with him. We talked for some time about the program and about where I was from. When I told him that I was visiting Camp Pendleton, he told me that I should get in touch with the Marine Band there and speak to the director. He gave me his phone number, and the next day, I broke from the group and got to spend some time with the Marine Band.

As it turned out, this became one of the most rewarding professional development activities of my career. They invited me to conduct the band at the noon rehearsal. We worked on several of the songs that would be played for the colors ceremony the next day. This event is the graduation ceremony for the current group of Marines who make it past basic training.

The best part of the whole experience happened next. The director of the Marine Band asked me to direct one piece of music in the ceremony the next day. As part of the ceremony, I received a picture of the event and a shirt to wear from the gift shop. I conducted "God Bless America" by Irving Berlin. It was an original, yellowed copy of the song that may have once been used in a performance for a president. That was what I had imagined anyway.

Conducting the Marine Band was an amazing experience but not quite as eventful as what happened earlier in the week. While I was in downtown San Diego one evening, I thought it would be a good idea to get a haircut. I was in an open-air mall and noticed a salon called Jocco's where at least ten amazingly beautiful women were cutting hair.

I made my appointment and sat in the waiting area for about fifteen minutes for my turn. I tried to guess which one of the nice young ladies would be cutting my hair. One of the girls came to get me, and we made our way over to one of the corner stations. I was so excited! This had been such a great trip. I just knew my wife would appreciate seeing me with a new haircut when I got home.

After my stylist had prepped me, she went around the corner to the back of the salon. A few minutes later, another hair stylist greeted me. I believed him to be Jocco, but I never was quite sure. He was a very large and flamboyant Mexican man with the biggest curly hair I had ever seen. Although I didn't have trouble with a Mexican man cutting my hair, the prospect of having my delicate hairs cut by Jocco himself was just not as pleasant as what I had first imagined. I wasn't sure what was going on, so I just sat back and let life happen.

The next twenty minutes taught me a few very valuable lessons. The first lesson is that Jocco—although not what I expected—could really cut hair well. He had some of the most interesting stories to tell. I looked even more beautiful than before and came away with a rich experience that I will always remember.

I also learned that the dreams I dream and the reality I live may not necessarily match. The important goal is making the most of each experience and enjoying the people I meet along the way. Individuals that cross my path may not always fit my ideal, but they will always teach me something new about myself. I can be sure that everyone has value, even if I cannot imagine what that value might be.

This trip was an outstanding opportunity. I learned so much from going on my journey, and when I got back to town, it was what I talked about to my kids for the next month. Just being able to see the Marine style of leadership was enough to make the trip invaluable to me. Conducting the Marine Band was the icing on the cake. Receiving a haircut from Jocco—priceless! These types of educational opportunities are just what it takes to improve your leadership style and give you a larger view of your world. A complete diary of this trip can be found on my web page: www.bolivarmusic.org.

Classroom Questions and Activities

1. List a few negative aspects of your own personality that need to change.
2. How is each of these personality traits likely to affect your classroom management?

This would be a great time to consider what I mentioned at the outset of this book. Please consider telling your friends about this book. You are my best and only hope for moving this book into the hands of those it will benefit most. Promoting a self-published work is difficult. With your help, this book can find its way into the hands of someone who needs it most—a new teacher.

7
Confusing Passion with Authority

"The more a man meditates on good thoughts, the better his world and the world at large will be." Confucius, 500 B.C.

In developing proper leadership, never confuse passion with authority. To be passionate about your program is an admirable quality but must be tempered by control of emotion. Passion and emotion go hand in hand. By keeping yourself calm and assertive and constantly checking your ego and emotions, you can confidently manage every situation in a professional manner and with a smile on your face. There is nothing more unnerving to a poorly disciplined student than to be corrected in an assertive manner by a smiling teacher who is in complete control of emotions.

Other than receiving your huge paycheck and the big raise you will get each year, attaining respect and admiration from students and parents is part of what every teacher wants most from a career in education. This can be lost in a single sentence when emotions are not in check. Knowing the difference between yelling and raising your voice is very important. Yelling at students to get what you want only leads to resentment and loss of respect. On the other hand, raising your voice to make a point is perfectly acceptable if you do it in a way that preserves dignity. If you cannot control your own emotions, you cannot expect to control the emotions of the students you lead. It is possible to be assertive without becoming a tyrant. Even in the worst of situations, being a tyrant is not effective.

Did you notice how the first sentence in the paragraph above made you feel? That little bit of humor took you by surprise and illustrates my point entirely. Emotion is a huge motivator and makes you believable. It shapes others' perception of you. If I had started the paragraph above in a different way, your attitude may have been completely different.

What if I had said it this way? "Most teachers hate their jobs because of poor pay. I guess gaining the admiration and respect from parents and students is all they have left." Wow! Using words differently completely changes the tone. You may have put the book down at that point and opened a jar of peanut butter (yummy peanut butter). See! I did it again. Now you feel butter, I mean better.

Remember, yelling is not the way you normally talk to people. Occasionally, someone says something, and you say to yourself, "That makes sense." This may happen when you hear what I am going to say next.

You do not normally yell at the people in your life. Would you yell at your spouse to get your way? You might, but you are taking your life into your own hands. Do you yell at your principal when you are frustrated? You might, but you would probably get fired, and you definitely wouldn't be getting that new smart board. The point is this: We take liberties with our students in the department of emotion that we would never take if the parents were in the back of the room.

Let me fill you in on a truth that may be hard for you to understand fully. This truth is obvious to a veteran teacher but may be missed entirely by a new teacher. The truth is this: **No negative or unsuccessful situation you face in the classroom is too great that it cannot be overcome by simply changing your approach or educational method.** By doing this simple step, you can completely solve the problem. Insulting or yelling at the student is merely movement in the opposite direction and ineffective as an educational method.

> "When it becomes obvious that your goals cannot be attained, don't adjust your goals. Instead, adjust the steps you take toward your goals." Confucius, 500 B.C.

In my early career, I would have rehearsals where I completely lost control of my emotions because students were not performing simple tasks. In these instances, it now becomes obvious that simply changing the approach would have made all the difference. By practicing the scale of the piece first, I may have avoided missed notes. By simply using a metronome, I could have allowed the students to keep a steady beat. The approach you choose can be the defining factor for success in your classroom.

While we are on the subject, how did you act the last time the principal was in the room observing you? Did you give more effort in being organized? Did you give more effort to your appearance, motivation, classroom organization, attitude, or attention to detail? I bet you, did and I bet the students acted better for you that day. Did you yell? I bet you didn't. Control your emotions, and you can control your class in a more efficient manner.

"No man can effectually instruct another without first having a reference to his own character and wishes." Confucius 500 B.C.

Classroom Questions and Activities

1. Tell a story about someone in your life who displayed a negative or harsh attitude. How did this harsh attitude make you feel? Share these stories with your group.

8
Shaping the Perception of Expectations

Many studies show us that expectations are based on perception. If a student is told that a highly complex task is difficult, failure will be a statistical certainty. If a student is told that a hard task is easy, research shows that the student is likely to succeed with ease. Perception is the key ingredient in the outcome.

When I started my career as a band director, one of my main challenges with beginning clarinet players was teaching them to cross the break. Crossing the break, or middle of the clarinet, involves the use of ten fingers on eleven keys. It is the single most difficult aspect of learning to play clarinet. My mistake came by telling the students that it was a difficult task. I said that we could work it out over time and get better. That is exactly what happened. It took too much time.

By changing my approach and telling them that it was as easy as pie, I found out that the students learned to do it much more quickly. I was creating a mental roadblock for them by saying that it was hard. A simple change in approach made all the difference.

Expectations are shaped by a student's previous successes or failures. Being successful in a task will breed the desire for more success and increase optimism in the activity. Failing at a set of tasks will ultimately breed fear of failure.

Many of the intricacies with motivation are tied to needs that may or may not be met at home by the family. Giving careful attention to a student's background can help you decide which tools to use to motivate in a given direction. Using the incorrect tools or making tasks too difficult, however, can be costly.

A more effective approach with a non-motivated student is to give him one easy task to complete that is related to the larger picture. After he completes that task, he has now gained momentum. Give him a push again and, before long, he is doing the entire multi-step task.

I had a trumpet player one year who was having trouble with a solo he was going to take to contest. We had just passed the new music out, and this student, last chair in his section, just sat there doing nothing. Other students were struggling through the first reading of the solo, but he sat there with an apathetic look on his face.

When I noticed this, my first reaction was to treat this situation as a discipline problem. He was, after all, just sitting there doing nothing. Upon questioning the student after class, I found out that his main concern was a high note in the first measure that he had never played. The fear of that note caused him to put the horn down on his lap and pout. While other students were playing the solo well, this student refused to get past the first measure.

I kept him for a few minutes after class and asked him if he would do something over the weekend. I simply asked him to play the note one octave lower from where it was written and even marked the note in the music for him. In the next rehearsal, not only was he playing the solo with the other students, he had managed to overcome his fear of the original note and was playing it as well as the others. One simple change made it possible for him to take the first step forward.

The most effective tool that you possess as an educator is the ability to shape perception. This ability is the driving force for shaping a student's thoughts and expectations about you, your classroom, and your program. **This type of positive perception leads to desire, with desire leading to seeking, and seeking finally leading to an increased velocity of movement toward success.** (See the chapter on Understanding the Underlying Causes of Misbehavior.)

On the flip side, by creating a negatively charged atmosphere, you create the same feelings and expectations among your students. This situation will lead to failure avoidance and can slow a student's momentum to a standstill. Constantly yelling, creating more rules to follow, pointing out students' flaws, and parading your negative perceptions around will only create an atmosphere of pessimism and give the students a reason to change direction away from where you want them to head.

You may be thinking that your classroom is so out of control that nothing will help. You may say that I have no clue when it comes to the kids in your classroom. That may or may not be true. I have taught in some tough situations and know first hand the fear that is generated by a harsh environment. The fact remains that you will succeed or fail by the choices you make, so make the best choices available. Creating a negative atmosphere can never help your unique situation, no matter how bad it is.

When I taught in southeast Missouri, I was in a school district that had a rough moral climate. I was in charge of ISS (in school suspension) for two hours a day with the worst of the worst. The kids in the room would intentionally serve out their time without bathing just to drive the supervisors crazy. To make matters worse, the room did not have a window. I normally sat my chair in the hall and looked into the room from there.

My first year as ISS supervisor was rough but improved greatly over the next two years. I was very negative and sour the first year, and I let it show to the students. I noticed there were days when I came in the room smiling from some great thing that had happened in my class the hour before, and the students in ISS responded with a more positive tone. Those days brought far less discipline issues to my attention. I was more inclined to joke with the kids and be less serious on those days.

It didn't take me long to figure out that if I was like this everyday, I would have a better time making it through to the second bell. I decided at this point to do an experiment. I came in one day very happy and tried to joke around with the kids as much as possible. I used humor, positive reinforcement in my reactions, and genuinely tried to find out what these kids were up to outside the walls of the school.

I learned more from my positive conversations in that room than I ever would have by being negative. We discussed their families, friends, and interests in a meaningful way. I used this information to lead the conversation toward their actions at school and their chances of success later in life. I made a point to get on the positive side of these students, and ISS became a place of personal growth for all of us.

When students come to crossroads in their lives, they have the following options: move ahead, go back, turn right or turn left to another activity, or simply stand still. By showing your positive optimism, you can help them continue forward. By being a negative pessimist, you give your students an option to change direction: move backwards or just stand still. If you want them to move forward with you, there is only one thing you can do: be positive and constantly optimistic. Your positive energy will show the way and might even reveal the hidden direction—up.

9
Classroom Management Routines

In the first part of this book, I have mainly discussed philosophical aspects of teaching style, behavior, motivation, leadership personality, and peanut butter (sorry, couldn't resist). While it is entertaining and beneficial to ponder these ideas, the real business of learning concrete classroom management techniques is most likely your main reason for reading this book.

The following chapters about teaching style should give you some of the techniques that you can use to develop a clear and consistent daily routine. Developing your own routine will be a huge investment in maintaining a calm classroom. These routines will ultimately give you what we are after—a chance to teach without distraction and to be free from the burden of stressful discipline issues while constantly motivating students to success.

Be aware of the fact that it may take time to solidify your classroom management skills. You will not get this into your psyche over night. Assimilating to a unique teaching style and routine takes practice and patience. Your constant, relentless, calm, and assertive optimism will remind you each day of what you are aiming for and will mold your perspective and ultimately your behavior as a world-class educator.

The twenty suggested routines that follow will assist you in maintaining consistent classroom management and large-group control. These routines are merely a good starting point for what I consider my best practices as a teacher. Use your own leadership style to develop additional routines that work for you.

The format for the following chapters will include tips on building leadership style in a concise manner. There will also be several examples and stories to illustrate how these routines have improved my teaching style over the last eighteen years. It will be important, as you read along, to think of specific instances from your own experiences. As you consider these experiences, focus on what you can improve about your own teaching style. You may find that some of these routines do not fit your personality. Take the routines that you find most useful, but be willing to try something new if you see a routine that you do not recognize.

Before you read the positive routines, realize that you can also have ineffective routines. Remember, your routines will make or break good classroom management. What follows is a list of routines to avoid. These are just a few of the many possibilities:

1. Ignoring small misbehavior and annoyances.
2. Constantly allowing students to speak their thoughts.
3. Allowing students to blurt out questions.
4. Taking your attention away from the class.
5. Beginning the lesson too soon, before attention is gained.
6. Losing focus of your lesson and drifting to unrelated topics.
7. Giving "free" time.
8. Teaching over distraction.
9. Having unclear expectations.
10. Being unprepared to teach the lesson.
11. Praising students for what is expected.
12. Not giving adequate praise to self-initiative.
13. Failing to plan ahead.
14. Spending too much time with one group and losing focus of the entire group.
15. Standing in one place for long periods of time.
16. Using a constant voice level.
17. Focusing too much on the negative.
18. Being too serious and stiff.
19. Avoiding humor.

20. Settling for less instead of expecting success.
21. Taking too much time explaining and spending too little time on engaging activities.

Use the list on page 116 for a handy reference of positive routines. Feel free to share the list.

Classroom Questions and Activities

1.   Which poor routines do you identify in your own personality?   How will you need to change for these to improve?

10
Routine #1: Eat Dark Chocolate

What's chocolate got to do with a routine you ask? Chocolate has everything to do with good classroom management. Look at chocolate as an example of a choice you can make to improve one small part of your health. Most educators, at least the educators I know, are coffee or soda drinkers. Ninety percent of Americans consume caffeine. Caffeine is the ultimate pick-me-up, right? Think again. Caffeine is a chemical molecule that acts on your central nervous system as a stimulant and makes you alert. It temporarily helps you to feel less drowsy. Good news, right? Not!

Caffeine actually makes you highly agitated, irritable, and nervous. It acts as a mild diuretic causing frequent urination. In times of high stress, caffeine exacerbates the feelings of being uncontrolled and can make you paranoid. For those of you who are also smokers, combine nicotine and caffeine, and you get a cardiovascular tsunami. Sounds like a winning combination. Put a slab of peanut butter on it, and it might make you at least feel better.

Dark chocolate, on the other hand, contains a molecule known as theobromine, which belongs with a class of alkaloid molecules similar to caffeine, known as methylxanthines. Theobromine, like caffeine, acts as a stimulant and an anti-depressant without the feelings of being anxious. But wait, there's much more.

Theobromine is similar to caffeine but on a lesser scale. Its effects last nearly twice as long as caffeine. It is used to treat high blood pressure, control the accumulation of body fluid, relieve dilation, and inhibit the proliferation of liver, colon, and gastric cancer cells. Chocolate is as healthy as anything you can consume, and its psychological benefits far outperform caffeine. It accomplishes this without any of the agitation or nervousness associated with caffeine consumption.

Here is a list of chocolate's benefits:

- Chocolate boosts energy.
- Chocolate is a stimulant that does not cause hyperactivity.
- Chocolate has sugar but is listed as a snack that is least likely to cause tooth decay.
- Chocolate contains Vitamins A1, B1, B2, C, D, and E.
- Chocolate contains magnesium, which has a whole host of health benefits.
- Chocolate contains phenylethylamine, which heightens mood.
- Chocolate contains tryphtophan, which is an amino acid that raises serotonin levels in the brain, which, oddly enough, lessens the craving of starchy foods.
- Chocolate contains a mono-unsaturated fat called oleic acid, which raises your good cholesterol and lowers your bad cholesterol.
- Chocolate prevents heart disease by helping your cells resist free radicals.

Recent finding presented by the American Association for the Advancement of Science (AAAS) confirms what chocolate lovers have known all along. Chocolate is good! The benefits listed above are only a few of the healthy side effects of a balanced diet that includes wholesome foods like chocolate. Studies continue to confirm the health benefits of chocolate, so eat up.

The main point here is that your diet can play an important role in starting your day. Eat some chocolate and get off the cigarettes and caffeine. Lose some weight. Do what you can to enhance your personal appearance. Do anything that will help you be a calm and assertive leader in your classroom. Change your diet, and you can add one quality that is more positive to your overall persona.

Classroom Questions and Activities

1. Describe your current diet.

2. What parts of this diet need to be improved?

3. Develop a long-range goal for yourself concerning your current diet.

11
Routine #2: Wake Up and Get Some Sleep

If you are tired right now reading this book, chances are your body is exhausted by stress, possibly agitated by caffeine, and tired from the fatigue of fighting through your day. When you are tired, you starve the brain of its ability to make strong decisions. Being calm and assertive suddenly turns into being tired and grumpy.

It is important for a calm and assertive leader to be focused. When you lose sleep, you lose focus. Lack of sleep can cause you to be irritable and out of control with your emotions. Without even realizing it, your negative perception of what is happening in your classroom could be directly tied to your lack of rest.

Have you ever noticed that on the nights you get good sleep, your students seem more calm and productive? Odds are that nothing has changed apart from the fact that your brain is more capable of handling its duties when you are rested. Your students' behavior will always reflect yours. If you want this reflection to be pleasing to you, then make sure you are rested.

Sleep is the brain's way of rebooting and sifting through the complex emotions of the day's activities, allowing it to be ready for the challenges of the next day. If you starve the brain of this rest, you will handicap your efforts in the classroom. Add caffeine to the mix, and you continue an endless cycle of fatigue and poor judgment. Build up enough days of this, and you can guarantee that major mistakes will be made. Jobs are lost from less than this, so wake up and get some sleep!

It is not enough to get just one good night of sleep. How many of us try to get to bed at a reasonable hour Monday through Thursday and then stay up all night on Friday and Saturday? You think that getting to bed on Sunday night early or napping all day Sunday afternoon will make things okay. Wrong!

Try something for six weeks, and I will guarantee you that you will have a new perspective on life. For the next six weeks, get regular sleep and starve your body of caffeine. Instead, eat dark chocolate that is marked 60% cocoa. Don't just eat dark chocolate though. Eat a school soy burger or two and some green beans. (You know they're your favorite).

Realize that some chocolates contain caffeine, so try to find a brand that does not have caffeine on the label. Make sure you eat chocolate anytime you feel like you have a headache from caffeine withdrawal, but make sure you never consume sweets or chocolate after mid-afternoon. This will give the chocolate a chance to clear your system so you can get to bed easily. Green or white tea can also be a good way to transition to a caffeine-free diet. They contain less caffeine than soda or coffee and contain similar properties to chocolate.

The first week will be the most difficult. Make sure that you get to bed early. Get to bed at the exact same time each night, and if you have trouble falling asleep, go ahead and just lie there. Your body will get needed rest, and you might have a chance to think without interruption. Make sure you don't think about school before you get to sleep. Think about your hobby, about an upcoming vacation, or about that sexy new copy machine in the attendance office. Relax! It's your time to rest and get away from it all. Make sure you do this all seven days of the week for six weeks.

After a week goes by, you will notice your craving for caffeine, and the accompanying sick and grumpy feeling you get, will fade. As more time passes, you will notice your sleep deepens, and you feel more refreshed in the morning. The best part is you will enjoy Mondays as if you were on summer break.

As the six weeks pass, the greatest benefit will be the increased feeling of control. Suddenly, being calm and assertive is not so hard. Your entire perspective on life will shift. Notice that I did not say change; I said shift. There is a difference. When your perspective changes, you have a change of heart, but when your perspective shifts, it is a change in your thinking. Your intellect will be telling you that the shift in perception is a good thing. This will be something you know is right instead of something you "feel" is right.

Do you remember when Homer had his epiphany in *The Simpsons Movie*? That's what I'm talking about! Homer had a shift in his perception about the problem he was having with his family. It brought him to the larger realization of his overall usefulness to society and that he was capable of overcoming his own weaknesses. Homer can be such a good role model.

Here are a few of the health benefits to quality rest:
- Reduced stress
- Increased alertness
- Improved memory
- Stronger immune system
- Improved productivity
- Improved physical appearance
- Healthier heart
- Improved brain power and comprehension
- Improved coordination
- Heightened mood
- Longer life

As you can clearly see, my claims in the introduction for better health were not some sort of trick after all. The truth is that health is a major factor in your life. Taking your health seriously and being health conscious is one more tool you can add to your belt. Your family will thank you forty years from now when you are still around to influence their own success. The grandchildren of your students will thank you when they step into your classroom. You'll be so healthy you'll never want to retire.

"Choose the vocation you love and you will never work a day in your life." Confucius 500 B.C.

Classroom Questions and Activities

1. Keep a log of your sleep habits for the next two weeks. Note your mood in even intervals throughout the day. Share this log with the group at the end of two weeks.
        a. For a real challenge, follow the sleep habits and diet restrictions from the last two chapters.

2. Write a brief paragraph or two describing how your sleep habits need to improve.

12
Routine #3: No Ideal

"Do not impose on others what you yourself do not desire." Confucius, 500 B.C.

Before class starts each day, imagine what you want your classroom to look like and expect it. Recall what I said in an earlier chapter. *"The most effective tool that you possess as an educator is the ability to shape perception."* The sum total of who you are is made up of what you spend your time thinking about. If you focus on what you want your class to look like and act on those thoughts, you will eventually see that what you imagine becomes reality.

What does the ideal classroom look like for you? We all have a vision of what we want our class to look like, smell like, and feel like. That's why we decorate, make bulletin boards, and hang student work. Be proud of what you are doing and make sure you keep your environment organized.

Are materials readily available? You need to have everything ready when you start your day. Fumbling around to make copies, find materials, or fiddling with technology is frustrating. Make it a habit to have everything readily available and set for action.

I can recall one year when I was really adding the technology to my two classrooms. We had just finished a fundraiser and used the money to install projectors, screens, and new computers. I looked around at the room; there was technology everywhere, wires hanging all over, remotes everywhere, and nothing was organized. I decided at that point to put it all in one place.

With the help of my assistant director, I used my experience in woodworking and cabinetry to build a new workstation that held all the new equipment in one place. I hooked up each piece of video hardware to a master selector and connected all audio to an inexpensive PA with wireless microphone. I made sure that each component worked from that moment forward.

Wow! What a huge change in my teaching. That year proved to be a giant leap in my students' performance and understanding. We incorporated specialized software to teach beginning band, and we used online resources to motivate and excite our students.

Once you have your classroom organized the way you want, check your room for safety. This is a huge issue when forming your ideal classroom and making it an effective reality. Students should feel that your classroom is warm and inviting. There should be no fear of contracting disease, being beaten by another student, or being bullied by the class clown. When you have your room organized for safety, you build your students' trust in you as a leader.

Another consideration is how your desks are placed. In my classroom, this is done by placing the students logically to maximize sound quality. Instrument grouping and placement is a huge deal with a band. How they sound to the audience and to the director depends on good placement.

I have three oboes in beginning band this year. Have you ever heard an oboe—a beginning oboe with a soft reed? How can I describe the sound? It's just like screaming monkeys in heat. Until an oboe player learns proper technique, everyone suffers.

As with any instrument, placement of the oboes is a big consideration. Some days I want to put the oboes out in the hall with duct tape over their mouths, but normally I place them behind the rest of the band until they gain control of their sound. I take great care in making sure their placement produces optimal results for the enjoyment of the audience and the pain it causes my ears.

Placement is important, but not nearly as important as the steps that are taken next. My normal procedure with a new oboe player is to find a double reed instructor to give them specialized assistance. As time passes, typical oboists learn to shave their reeds and gain control of their airflow. Before long with the proper guidance, they slowly develop vibrato and a characteristic tone quality. This does not come overnight, and the steps taken by me along the way are critical to movement forward for the oboist.

Imagine what you might do to make the classroom a better place and then act. Think about how changes could benefit the students in a positive way, and then make it happen. Use your best skills, and draw on the skills of others to get things organized.

You might build a book-reading loft, organize your chairs in a certain way, buy some cabinets, or pick a different color for the walls. The point is this: Do anything you can to make your room a happier, safer, and more productive place for kids to learn. Have an idea and be the first in your hall to be amazing. Watch all the other teachers copy your ideas.

One way to make the world a better place is to recommend a good book to a friend. Any good book will work. Take this book, for instance. This book would be a great book to recommend to a friend.
www.superiored.com

13
Routine #4: Full of Clutter and Confusion

As mentioned earlier, if you keep your classroom organized, you will feel better about your job, and your students will enjoy your class. A disorganized classroom speaks volumes about you as a teacher. Parents and students will judge your character as an educator. Whether you know it or not, students and parents form opinions about you and share those opinions with everyone they know.

It might be Christmas break, and the family is around the dinner table talking about their teachers. Your name comes up, and someone says, "Oh yeah, he's so disorganized." Perception is now locked in the minds of the audience that heard that comment, and it soon spreads. Before long, you become known by these conversations.

Having consideration for where kids come from is also a necessary aspect of being an educator. Kids may live in a mess at home, so coming to a clean and well thought-out classroom will be a welcome change to their lives. Your class may be one of the only places they go that shows them how to be organized. This may be one little thing you do that inspires the same from your kids. What would the same Christmas dinner conversation sound like in this situation?

The perception of others about your teaching style also applies to your administration. It is necessary to pay close attention to your school administration's policies on attendance, behavior, grading scale, and other duties that are required by your district. It is easy to lose a job when you are not organized enough to do the simplest tasks. Do you need an example?

I had a very large seventh grade band class one year. We were in our first week of school, and there was a drummer in the group who was very quiet. She never caught my attention in the classroom, and one day, she decided to skip class. I didn't catch it, so she decided to take the next few weeks off from my class to be in the nurse's office. I assumed that she had dropped the class and never double-checked.

To my embarrassment, she was called to the office one day. The kids told me that she had not been in our class for two weeks. I panicked and could not imagine why I had missed her on my roll sheet. We later found out what had been happening. Luckily, I was not the only teacher who made this mistake. After that day, I made it a point to be vigilant in this area. It makes me shudder to think how this could have turned out. Work hard to avoid the embarrassment that can come from these situations.

Here is a funny story that relates to confusion. My wife loves to tell this story to everyone we meet. Our second son came into the world and, as often happens, developed severe diaper rash. My wife had recently heard of a new product, Boudreaux's Butt Paste, and just knew this would do the trick. She sent my eldest son and me to the store to see if we could find this miracle cure. We made a few stops in the store and finally made our way to the medicine aisle.

We went up and down that aisle but could not quite remember the name of the product we needed. We brainstormed for a few minutes and continued to search. We finally came to a product that we thought was just what Mom asked for.

We returned home with our sack and proudly presented our purchase. Our youngest son had been crying since we left, and my wife was eager to put the product to the test. She opened the bag, and I will never forget—or live down—what came next. She reached into the bag and pulled out Zim's Crack Cream. She immediately started laughing until she cried. To make matters worse, our entire family was there to witness the blessed event. I was embarrassed and have continued to be embarrassed each time the story is told.

The moral to the story is simple: when you need to remember something as important as Boudreaux's Butt Paste, write it down! Believe me, the alternative is not worth the embarrassment. I did find out later that Zim's Crack Cream does wonders for dry hands after working with concrete. Who would have guessed?

As well as organizing yourself and your classroom, it is also your responsibility to assist your students with their organizational skills. I will never forget a history teacher I had in ninth grade. I was making very poor marks in my classes, and I was not motivated in any other class besides my father's band class. My history teacher made all of us take our notebooks out and said that he was going to give us a gift. We were all excited. What could this gift be, and why am I staring at my notebook? Was this some sort of trick?

He had us draw a line in the middle of the page from top to bottom and then another line at the top from left to right. He told us that this would guarantee higher grades in all our classes if we learned to take what he called "T-Notes." He said it with such conviction that I believed every word. We were told to put the teacher's words into the form of a question on the left and then answer the question on the other side.

What an incredible boost to my understanding. I took notes this way in all my classes. I started to get connected with what was being taught, and my grades went up. My parents were amazed at my new progress. Straight C's at last!

Another boost to my grades came my sophomore year in high school. My sociology teacher, who was also a coach, taught us sociology through discussion. He was very crafty in the way he brought out the information in our textbook. Through our discussions, I had suddenly discovered a subject that sparked my imagination. On game days, he would take us to the library to read. It didn't matter to him what we read, just that we didn't bother him. To me, this was another great part of his class.

I was browsing in the psychology section and came across *How to Win Friends and Influence People* by Dale Carnegie. That was just the magic book of tricks I needed to give me a larger view of my world. I suddenly realized that I could take charge of my circumstances by just doing a few things differently.

Deep down, I really did want to succeed. My problem at that time was that I felt dumb in all my classes. Sociology suddenly made me feel like I was smart in something. This belief became a boost to my self-esteem and I started feeling good about my classes. The book I discovered gave me a more organized way to approach my education.

The next day, I moved to the front in all my classes, started asking questions, smiled every once in a while, and tried to make my teachers feel important and admired. I was the teacher's pet in every class. My grades went to A's and B's, and I suddenly knew every detail of my teachers' families and hobbies. What a miracle this book was to my life. Not only did my teachers notice me; now I was suddenly connected to what they were teaching.

I tell you these personal stories to point out the fact that you have the power as an educator to enhance the life of a child. Your classroom organization is only a small part of the larger puzzle. Bringing all of your abilities and routines together can help you inspire a young mind to succeed, and being organized can only make this easier for you to accomplish.

It is very interesting to remember these experiences from my childhood. Learning to take T-notes from a history teacher and reading a silly little book on business success ended up developing a passion within me, which ultimately allowed me to be successful as a teacher. These seemingly insignificant events gave me the opportunity to flourish in my classes and graduate from college with a degree in Music Education. I owe it all to a couple of amazing teachers who were not afraid to inspire a young mind.

Classroom Questions and Activities

1. Describe your vision of the ultimate classroom.

2. Write a brief story about the teacher who influenced you most when you were young.

Studies show us that word of mouth is the best way to sell a product. Take this book, for instance. If only a few mavens decide to tell ten friends about this book, odds are that each of those ten will tell ten more friends. If my math is correct, and it's probably not, we are talking about slightly more people than all the editorial mistakes and poor examples of comma usage contained within this book. Using circular logic, we can conclude that if enough people buy this book, odds are good that a major publisher will publish this literary masterpiece and fix all those editorial mistakes. Everyone benefits.

www.superiored.com

14
Routine #5: Measure Twice, Teach Once

"Simply making excellent rules will not place you in a position of honor. Without honor, you cannot command credibility. Without credibility, your rules will not be followed. Therefore, your rules are rooted in your own character and conduct." Confucius 500 B.C.

"Have a set of simple rules displayed in your classroom." How many times have you heard those words come from the principal's mouth? Constantly reminding students of expectations is very important. It is never enough to read rules one time and then forget they are there. You need to live by your own rules.

I consider my rules black and white with a few shades of gray. I find this to be very effective. You can never enforce rules as if there are no other possibilities. If we all did this, "I'll let you off with a warning this time" would never be heard from an officer again. I don't know about you, but I need to hear that often.

If you choose to be only black and white with your discipline, be prepared for the consequences. When you consider rules to be black or white, being consistent is much more of an issue. Black and white means good and bad students are punished equally, no matter the circumstance. There are no exceptions. If you are not prepared to follow through with this, you will be seen as inconsistent. This creates more problems than it solves.

Traffic court is a perfect example of how this can work. Your driving record will tell the judge how lenient or strict he should be with your case. If you already have four points on your license and you get another speeding ticket, watch out. If you have a perfect driving record, you may only get a warning. If this is the way it works in life, it should work this way in your classroom.

With that said, there are some violations of the law that will not allow you to get by with a warning. It should be the same in your classroom. A student may bully another student within your view. In this case, you have no choice but to calmly take the student to the office and visit with the principal. There are many situations where this will be true, and it is imperative you know the difference. Understanding your school's code of conduct and having a grasp on state law will assist you in making solid disciplinary decisions.

Even if you have some gray areas, do not bend rules. Instead, make the same rules for everyone, and then choose wisely when you decide to reinforce them with punishment. I give students a few warnings before my basic rules become black and white. I look for patterns of behavior instead of specific instances and constantly redirect. It is a huge motivator for anyone to think that a favor is being given or when someone thinks so highly of them that they are willing to let something go one time. We all love it when this happens. Just make sure you do not damage your credibility.

Having one rule for one student and different rules for another will damage your credibility and will warrant hard feelings from the parent. Make sure your students know that the rules are to be followed by everyone, and then use your own judgment on how far you go before you punish a student for repeated misbehavior. Let students know up front that you are checking for patterns of behavior and not just specific instances. That way, they know where you stand. If you prefer to be stricter with your discipline, then remember to be consistent and willing to punish the best students as well as the worst equally.

Another very important consideration is determining who is to blame for a classroom problem. You may have a rule that says, "You must put your folder away each day when class is over." If you constantly see folders left out and never say anything about it, then who is to blame for ten folders on the floor each day? It is easy to say the kids, but ultimately, you are the one in charge.

The best solution is to remind students individually and then set guidelines for further infractions. This lets the student know that he is on notice for his behavior. Then, if the behavior continues, you must follow through with your expectations. If you do not follow through, you will lose all credibility. The problem of folders being left out will continue. If you go overboard and lose control, you will harm your relationship with the students and throw away your chances of success.

If there is a pattern in classroom misbehavior by large groups of students, the problem is normally your lack of communication or something missing in your classroom organization or routine. Do not be too quick to say, "The kids should know better." They should know better, and you need to be the one to ensure that they do. Blame yourself if the problem starts with you, and be willing to adapt your procedures before blaming the students.

A good example of this happened to me at a Christmas concert. I received an email from a parent about how good the concert was but that she was disappointed in the behavior of the sixth grade students when they were sitting together in the audience. My assistant director and I were on stage and could not see what the kids were doing. We were too busy conducting and setting the stage between groups.

This is clearly an example of poor planning on my part. I should have made sure there were teachers available to monitor this large group of sixth graders. I also should have made sure my expectations were clear from the beginning. I assumed that the students would behave since they had been good in the classroom. My assumption was incorrect.

In this situation, the students should not be punished. Punishment is not appropriate if the teacher could have prevented the problem from happening in the first place. The best course of action would be to let the students know how you feel about their poor behavior and give them clearer expectations in the future. It would be a fantasy to think that sixth graders would behave without supervision and, somehow, behave the next time if they were punished. This method will only set you up for more disappointment in the future.

It is your job as a teacher to foresee problems before they happen and adapt your procedures and expectations to avoid these issues. By finding the root cause of misbehavior, you can determine the best course of action. It is always important to recognize when your lack of good management has allowed room for misbehavior to occur. Developing effective rules and routines will minimize the potential for individual misbehavior and therefore minimize damage to the dignity of the student.

Continual misbehavior is the last issue that I would like you to consider. How many times have you scanned your classroom, noticed a student doing something that is contrary to your wishes, and ignored the behavior? This is easy to do when you are busy trying to teach and stressed by your classroom demands.

You may think that you are accomplishing more by keeping your focus on the lesson, but ignoring constant misbehaviors, even small ones, will ultimately cause you stress and grief. It is important to have good routines in place and ensure that your ideal classroom is realized each day with consistency. If you can narrow your behavior problems down to the smallest issues, the larger issues will disappear.

Classroom Questions and Activities

1. Develop a list of rules to use in your classroom.

2. Share your list of rules with the class and discuss.

15
Routine #6: Hey You!

At the beginning of each class, make sure you gain attention. Use any means necessary to bring the focus of attention to you.   Once all your routines are firmly established, you will only need to stand up in front of the class with a raised hand to hear the hum of the lights and the pitter-patter of little brains.

If you are considering ways to gain attention, you need to look no further than your computer screen or television. How does a webmaster drive attention to his website?   The answer is content. If your website has not been updated for three months, odds are people will stop visiting.   If you constantly add more content, you will have lots of attention from your viewers.   By adding attractive content to your delivery, you will succeed in drawing attention your way.

Have you ever thought about using advertising tactics in your lessons? We have our attention drawn to companies all the time by advertising. The next time you give your students closing comments for the day, try adding a hook. A "hook" is an advertising term that refers to the part of the advertising that gains attention, the part that reels you in. Build a desire for something important that will happen the next day, and then remind the students at the beginning of the next day about that thing. You instantly have their attention, and the excitement level is now elevated.

The other day, my assistant director walked out for a moment as I was telling the kids to use the power of association. It was the topic in our lesson. I was trying to get them to associate the key signature of natural minor with its relative major key. I told them that when they got home and opened the refrigerator, let that be their reminder to write hello on a piece of paper and then bring it back to school the next day and hand it to the assistant director. They all did it. Hello papers showered the assistant director.

This turned out to be a fun activity that allowed me to easily gain attention in class and illustrate a valuable lesson with association.

A few years ago, I was searching for an idea to get students to visit our music department website. I came up with the idea of adding a hidden page, which was hyperlinked to a period at the end of a sentence. I then added fake leads to other places around the website that would throw kids off the trail. We told the kids to search the web page for the hidden link. The first student to email me with the answer to the question on the hidden page got a king-sized candy bar as a prize. We had thousands of hits that month until someone finally found the hyperlinked period.

Here is another story that illustrates my point beautifully. I was in the last week of rehearsals with my seventh grade band, and the students were repeating the same mistakes that they had made for the last month. We would rehearse a section and have it perfect at the end of rehearsal only to make the same mistakes in the next rehearsal. It was very frustrating.

I was home one evening reading a book on philosophy when I came across an old Greek myth about a man named Sisyphus. The thought occurred to me that this might be a wonderful illustration to use in class. I searched the internet and located a short, animated video of Sisyphus that could aid in my delivery.

We were preparing to begin rehearsal the next morning, and the students were busy moving to their seats. I had the video paused and waiting. My introduction explained that I had an interesting video to show the class about a man who had a problem. As the video played, I explained that this man, Sisyphus, was condemned by the gods to roll a rock up a hill, only to have the rock fall back down again each time he reached the peak. He was forced to repeat this process for eternity.

As the students watched the cartoon, I went on to point out how the actions of Sisyphus related to our recent rehearsals. I had their perfect attention, and my point could not have been made any stronger. The students drew from this experience in the rehearsals that followed, and we had an amazing performance a week later. Now, merely mentioning the name of Sisyphus draws on a memory of an entire story and in one minute says more than I could say in twenty.

Use your own ideas to gain attention and make sure these ideas focus on a valuable outcome. Gaining attention is a necessary part of teaching and complements strong leadership. Be creative with your approach and add one more tool to your belt.

Classroom Questions and Activities

1. Develop five unique ways to gain attention in a classroom.

2. Develop a unique lesson plan similar to the ideas described in this chapter. Share your ideas with the class.

16
Routine #7: Weapons of Mass Distraction

After gaining attention, stop all distractions before you consider teaching or moving forward with any activity. It is easy to get caught up in what you are doing and teach over these distractions, so avoid this at all costs. Even if it takes ten minutes, put out discipline fires, and constantly redirect students to make eye contact with you. Give them good reasons to look at you, and be relentless. Redirect behavior as needed, and remain calm and assertive at all times. Remember that you are the one in charge. It will become much easier to eliminate distractions once you make this a part of your teaching routine.

One particularly effective way to eliminate a room full of distractions is to use students' first and last names when addressing behavior. If you correct one student by their full name, even if twenty kids are being a distraction, the one name you call is as good as calling all the names at once. If one person is in trouble, the rest will instinctively stop for fear that they will be next. The student who was called will be completely connected to you after he hears the room go quiet. Make sure to select the most deserving student, and never use the same student for this more than once in a day. If you find yourself calling the same student, then you are facing willful misbehavior. This must be corrected immediately. If you allow these types of misbehaviors to occur, this then becomes your routine. Remember that it is possible to have bad routines.

In a large-group setting, a distraction like a knock on the door, the intercom, a broken instrument, or a phone call can completely destroy your class if your focus is taken away from your routine. In a small class, if you need to get off the task of teaching for a few minutes, you can assign busy work and go on with life. If you are in charge of a large group, this is entirely a different matter.

In a large group, it is best to have a plan mapped out for every possible distraction using student leadership. Assign trusted students to aid you in intercepting distractions like phone calls or guests at the door. By doing this, you avoid breaking your routine.

There are other distractions that are worth considering, and you may not even be aware that they are present in your classroom. Go into your classroom for an hour when it is quiet. Listen to the sounds you hear around you. Does your air conditioning or heating system kick on and rattle? Do your desks squeak? Is your fish tank bubbling loudly? Does your small refrigerator make noise? Are there objects in your room that could be repaired to eliminate noise? These are all sounds that you may be drowning out from your own consciousness, but your students may find them distracting. Finding ways to eliminate noise may be beneficial in small ways.

There are several noises in my band classes that I must constantly work to eliminate. Students have a tendency to hum along with the music that they have just heard. They mean well and are just happy, but it is a distraction nonetheless.

Another noise I deal with is clicking drumsticks. This is simply nervousness and high energy from a drummer who needs constant stimulation to remain in control. I try to redirect the behavior to the legs so that the student is still rehearsing their part and being active in a way that is quiet.

Students in band have a tendency to keep their cases under their chairs. Once I noticed that this was a constant source of noise, I made the students aware that they need to keep the cases away from their feet. This eliminates the chance for the cases to become a source of distraction.

Imagine all of the things that a band director could face when it comes to this idea of noise in the classroom. Students in a band class are sitting behind a large metal object with a W.M.D. (weapon of mass distraction) in their hands, confined into a small area with other students, and constantly bombarded by a fast and energetic stimulus. This is a formula for disaster if the teacher is not in control of his class.

It is vital for the one in charge to have a grip on all distractions in the room. Ensuring that students are self-controlled when it comes to distraction is paramount to the success of the activity. Another area that relates to this concept will be found in the next chapter. Considering the ideas found in these two chapters will become central to your overall ability to control your classroom.

Classroom Questions and Activities

1.   Think of five other ways that distractions could be eliminated in a classroom. Share your ideas with the class. Are there pitfalls with your approach?

17

Routine #8: Hunting for Abrupt Verbal Commentary

This routine is utterly and completely vital. I cannot stress this to you enough. The single most annoying aspect of teaching is the constant blurting out of useless banter among students. Immaturity, especially between sixth and ninth grade, can drive you to insanity as a teacher. Minimizing this aspect of your day is of utmost importance. Many of the procedures for good classroom management that I promote in this book will be useless without observing this routine.

All abrupt verbal commentary from students must be constantly ignored and redirected to a raised hand. Never let a student interrupt you with commentary, jokes, or questions. Never answer a student who interrupts. The only answer is, "I only speak to a raised hand." I learned that phrase from my wife.

You will be tempted to break this routine. When something incredibly funny is said by a student, it's hard not to join in. When someone asks a good question, it is hard not to answer. As an effective teacher, you will naturally want to give an answer to a good question. To be consistent, you need to be serious about this routine and keep control based on this expectation. Let up one time, and you lose control. You might as well go behind your desk and hide because you will not be teaching in an environment where the kids control the classroom.

Some teachers may think this is too strict. This might be true in certain circumstances like group discussion where you want ideas and debate to flow. The way around this is to announce that your expectation is being set aside for now so the discussion can take place. That way, your normal expectation of a quiet class is preserved and reinitiated with little effort.

In a large group such as a band or choir, this cannot be done without getting out of control. In large groups, two people have the floor at a time. The teacher and the student who is recognized to talk should be the only two talking. Keep it quick, and move on to the next student.

I can tell you from experience that it is much better to keep students from feeling free to say what they think than to let them feel free to express their thoughts at random. I have tried it both ways and every which way you can imagine. I have experimented with every conceivable policy for student talking. I came to this conclusion: there must only be two people able to talk at any given moment. This is the least frustrating method for students who have not developed the self-control necessary to maintain their communication with common sense.

As a classroom teacher for a small class, you will decide this for yourself based on each particular class you see. If you have trouble with disruption from students, the guidelines I have listed above will help you gain control. If your students are capable of communicating with control, then you can relax this restriction to help make the class more enjoyable. With practice, this can be turned on and off like a faucet.

The year I realized the importance of this routine was the year I saved myself as a teacher. Stopping abrupt verbal commentary from happening in a classroom takes constant vigilance but pays off big in then end. Just think of how great your year would be if all the teachers in your district knew about this simple routine and practiced it consistently. Humm... If only there was some magic device that could send them all a message at the same time telling them to buy this book.

www.superiored.com

18
Routine #9: Look, Candy!

When a small child is causing you a problem, pulling out a piece of candy can move the original focus in a different direction, therefore eliminating your problem. This is called redirection. The basic idea is to find an alternative direction that draws the target away from the undesired behavior. Redirecting a behavior takes a bit of skill and imagination, but the rewards of this routine can be immense.

Last Christmas, I was sitting in my mother's living room working on this book. My nephew Dion was sitting on the floor playing quietly. Without warning, he got up and started banging on the piano. Needless to say, this was disrupting my thought process.

My solution was to sit on the floor and begin playing with one of his toys in a loud manner. This redirected Dion back to the floor for another fifteen minutes. We repeated this process until I was finished with what I was doing. This is a perfect example of redirection.

Redirect behavior, and make it a constant part of your teaching style. To redirect behavior, you simply take the direction that a behavior is headed and push it a different way, either by body language, use of words, or by redefining your instructions. Redirecting behavior most often avoids the need for abrasive comments that cause feelings of failure in the child. When redirecting does not work or last very long, then disciplinary measures that are more drastic will be necessary. See the chapter *Dealing with Willful Misbehavior.*

Kids do not always understand why they misbehave. You must remember that students do not act—they react. These reactions may not have anything to do with you or your class. These reactions can arise from what happened in the class before, from the hallways, from feelings of failure, from boredom, or from your lack of communication. They may even come from feelings caused by an abusive parent. Any number of causes is possible. Redirecting these reactions to a positive outcome should be your first choice when dealing with classroom problems.

Keep in mind that redirecting behavior is not your only choice. A well-trained classroom manager will have an entire bag of tricks when dealing with misbehavior. Using a varied style will be helpful when redirecting is ineffective.

It is also worth noting that your perception of the discipline problem may not be the perception of the student. You may see a defiant student while the student sees his actions as normal behavior. What you consider disruptive may be perfectly acceptable at home. What you see as laziness may simply be a lack of stimulation from the family or just simply the student's inability to perform. Remember that failure is not nearly as fun as destroying the teacher and succeeding at it. How you proceed can be enhanced by first knowing why the student behaves the way he does.

I had a trombone player one year who had a very loud voice. He talked so loudly that his deep voice could be heard from two hallways away. You know the kind of kid I am talking about—high energy and high volume. It was not too long before I was calling home to explain to the mother how I would like this student to calm down a bit. When I made the call, I discovered something that helped me deal with the problem.

After a brief conversation with his mother, I discovered that he was from a family of nine. During the entire phone conversation, I could barely make out what was being said for all the people in the background yelling and laughing. These people were happy and loud! The next day, I told the student that I realized he was from a large and loud family. I simply asked him to do me a favor and keep it down in my class, and I would appreciate him for it.

That was it. My approach made all the difference. He is in my high school band now and still being very quiet. He is the kind of student I would have dropped from my band ten years ago. Now he is a productive member of the trombone section.

Imagine for a minute that I had yelled at him in class and challenged him to a shouting match. Would things have turned out differently?

Classroom management is all about perspective and approach. Most people are basically good inside and want to be liked. No matter how their actions contradict this, it is true nonetheless. How you choose to deal with a given situation can be improved by considering perspective and approach. Instead of insulting self-esteem, redirect the behavior to a positive outcome for both you and the student and make sure you research the root cause of the issue.

Some misbehavior that you encounter cannot be redirected. This behavior should be considered disrespect. Disrespectful misbehavior, for the most part, is merely the student's unconscious way of testing your reactions. If you are calm, consistent, and assertive, then little room is left for this kind of behavior. By taking this approach, you may contribute positively to the student's personality and allow them room to grow.

There is one last consideration with redirecting behavior that can be very effective. Using a slight bit of humor in your redirection can calm and disarm a student and will preserve the relationship you have with that student.

When you feel like a student is pushing back at you, try to inject some humor to lighten the mood. If this is ineffective, you have just discovered something about his character that needs to be addressed in a different way. Here, redirecting his behavior may not be effective because the problem originates outside the classroom. A different approach may be necessary.

Redirecting behavior is important when considering your classroom expectations. The expectations you have for your students should not be overshadowed by distraction. Directing students toward your expectations will be a constant battle. This battle will only be won through your constant focus and attention. We will cover this further in the next chapter.

Classroom Questions and Activities

1. List five examples of redirection. Be creative. Compete with your class for the most creative example.

19
Routine #10: Expect More or Get Less

"In all endeavors, success depends on previous preparation. Without previous preparation, failure is certain. Think before you act and you will not stumble." Confucius, 500 B.C.

After students are calm, clearly define your expectations. As I have said before, your students need to know what you expect. This cannot be overstated. Much of their misbehavior can originate with your lack of expectations. If they know you have high expectations, they will give you what you expect and be so busy they cannot do anything else.

If you give partial or confusing directions, your students will give you partial effort. Put yourself in their shoes, and imagine what it is like to have unclear expectations. Have you experienced this from your administrators before? Have you ever received incomplete emails from people who presume you know what they are wanting? Too little information can be frustrating. You should always assume that your students do not know what you are saying. Your message must be communicated as thoroughly as possible.

Do not just say what you expect; define what you expect from students on a daily basis. This starts from the first day of class and continues until you are kicked back behind the barbeque grill in June. Define your expectations in detail, and be consistent.

Your expectations will be tied to your routine. If your actions do not convey the same message as your words, you will frustrate your students. I said earlier that it is very easy to slip into this habit of teaching over distraction. A student clicking a pen or banging his desk around is not something you should accept. Constantly reinforce your expectations, and do not show frustration. Be calm and assertive. **If you**

show weakness to your students, you give control to them. You must calmly assert yourself as the "one" in charge.

Notice I said "your" expectations in the paragraph above. The students will expect it if you do. You must be persistent and consistent. If you are not consistent, that tells the students that you have changed your expectations or worse, that your expectations are meaningless. Keep your expectations high and be persistent.

Once you have defined your expectations for your students, you may want to consider what expectation they have for you. Expectations Avenue is the hallway that goes past my band room—literally. Our former principal named all the hallways with street signs as part of his advertising campaign for success. Keep in mind that expectations are a two-way street. Your students will be just as disappointed in you as you are in them if expectations are not met.

As you develop your leadership style, remember that education is not about me; it's about we. If you miss appointments with students and cannot deliver on your promises, you take two steps back on your credibility as a leader. Lead yourself well if you expect to lead many well.

Classroom Questions and Activities

1. Create a sample list of expectations that you might use in your future classroom. This list of expectations can be similar to your list of rules. Some teachers prefer to have expectations rather than rules. Make sure your wording reflects an expectation and not a rule.

20
Routine #11: You Only See What You Are Prepared to See

"People only see what they are prepared to see." This quote from Ralph Waldo Emerson can be interpreted many ways. To me, it illustrates the lack of preparation a new teacher has when entering the classroom for the first time. You are only going to be aware of the problems that are familiar to you. Having open eyes when monitoring your classroom is not enough. Being prepared to understand what you see is therefore the goal.

This is also true for your students. The students' perspective about your classroom is guided by their understanding of what they see and hear from you. It is your responsibility as an educator to understand what you see when you scan your classroom. It is equally necessary to understand what your students see when they look across the classroom at you.

To ensure that you have an ideal environment, you must constantly monitor the classroom to make sure the students are on task and behaving. Students will behave and perform according to your expectations. If they believe that you do not see what they are doing, they will continue in the behavior. You need to be vigilant enough to see what is happening and communicate the fact that you know what the students are doing. Remember, you are the one in charge. They will not behave unless you demand it.

You should also constantly monitor for breaches in your routine. Let's say that you are telling a joke to your students, and it's really funny. You are on top of your game, and the thought occurs to you that this just might be the funniest thing that you have ever said. Suddenly, one of your kids in the class joins in and adds some abrupt humor. He disrupts what you are saying, stealing the moment away from you. As quickly as he disrupts class, five other students do the same. Your routine has suddenly been interrupted. What do you do at this point?

It is easy to join in and let the disruptive students take the floor from you. Keep consistent with your expectations for a quiet class, and redirect the students to raising hands to speak. Preserve your routine at all costs. If you do this consistently, you will find that these typical problems cease to happen.

It is also important not to lose focus on any area of the classroom or on any student. This is vital in large groups. Use the eyes in the front of your head, the back of your head, your peripheral vision, and any other body part to make sure that you always know what is happening in the room.

No matter how much you monitor your classroom, unexpected things will happen. "If they want you, they'll get you," as my brother-in-law says. Despite your best efforts and skills, there will be students who are capable of slipping past you.

This happened to me one day when I was teaching in Illinois. We had just finished a rehearsal, and I let the kids put their instruments away. Part of my routine at the end of the day is to have the students return to their original seats while waiting for the bell to ring.

The classroom that I was in had concrete and carpeted risers in three tiers that were shaped in arcs. We were there waiting, and I had placed myself at the top of the third tier where I could see what was happening around the room. The class was quiet. We had approximately one minute to go before the bell rang, and it seemed like any other day. This is where the story gets good.

I heard a commotion on the other side of the room, and suddenly there were flames rising five feet high around a group of students. I rushed over to see what was happening. Without hesitation, I told a student near the fire alarm to pull it as quickly as possible. She smiled really big and pulled the alarm like it was something she had always wanted to do.

The alarm was sounding, and all I could think about was getting the kids out of the room. The flames would not go out. It was as if I was stomping on napalm. One of my brighter students suggested that we somehow put the fire out. I thought about throwing a tuba player on the fire and having him roll around, but I hesitated. Instead, I grabbed a music folder and popped the flames with a sudden blow. This smothered the flames and finally put them out.

At this point, the entire school was out of the building, and the superintendent, who was also the principal, was on his way in. We stood there talking about what had happened. He was not kind to me with his speculation of what had gone on in my classroom. His gut reaction was to ask, "Where were you when this happened?" I stood my ground and told him that I was watching the entire class. I reminded him that the student who did this was supposed to be removed from my class the week before. Instead, he was sent to ISS and then placed back in my room a week later because he needed the credit to graduate. I also pointed out that the entire reason he was in our school district in the first place was because he had been expelled from the last school he attended for similar problems.

I later received an apology from the superintendent and new carpet in the band room. The old carpet was ugly green, torn, and it smelled like rotten eggs and fish. As for how the fire was started, the student was angry at being back in my class and decided that he would use some lighter fluid to start a little camp fire in the band room to make sure he was kicked out for good. After some mediation with a lawyer and his expulsion from our school district, I learned that I cannot see everything in my classroom, even by the light of a campfire, and you can never predict what will happen at any given moment.

Students can be unpredictable even when you watch their every move.

When monitoring your classroom, you should think about a few additional considerations. It is easy to ignore students who require help. There will be many reasons that students may require special attention, and you may not always understand why a question is important to the student. Realizing this fact will be important to leading your classroom well.

Do not get so wrapped up with your lesson that you forget to answer all questions. Parents can be angered when they hear that their little darling is not getting the attention she deserves. Be quick to answer questions, and do so in a way that keeps your routine in tact. Remember, there are no wrong questions, only wrong answers. Every question is important, and you should not make light of a student's lack of understanding.

Children can be concrete thinkers all the way up to the age of fifteen. It is not until around the age of twelve that they really begin to think in an abstract way. Very young students are less likely to infer meaning from your questions. There are plenty of good examples of this.

If you offer a small child the choice between a dime and a nickel, which will he choose? He will choose the nickel because it is larger. That is concrete thinking. You would choose the dime because it has more value. Abstract thinking involves looking at more than just the size of the coin.

Abstract thinkers can see relationships and attributes; whereas, concrete thinkers can only see what is most obvious. Therefore, a student's awareness of what is happening in the classroom may not be the same as your view of the classroom. Have compassion on their limited abilities and help them see the larger picture. Do not take it for granted that a student, especially a younger student, will understand what you are saying. You may see a dumb question as a discipline problem when it is really just concrete thinking. By answering the issue in a harsh manner, you create a feeling of failure in the student.

Understanding what you see when you monitor your classroom can be tricky. Your perception of what you see is critical to the choices you will make. Your understanding of the students' underlying motivations can assist you in determining which actions will be necessary when solving the unique problems you will face and the conflicts you will encounter. Your ability to mediate your decisions in these cases will be covered in later chapters.

As you consider your routines, recognize that they are interrelated and dependant on the others for success. As you continue to read, make the necessary connections between routines and recognize how one affects the other. How do these routines succeed or fail in your own leadership style?

Classroom Questions and Activities

1. What are five aspects of education that you may be unprepared to see with clarity?

21
Routine #12: Are You Easy on the Eyes?

"I hear and I know. I see and I remember. I do and I understand." Confucius, 500 B.C.

If students are going to hear what you are saying, eye contact must consistently be directed toward you at all times. When you notice any student looking anywhere besides your direction, stop and address the issue as fast as possible. Remember, students cannot talk if their eyes are focused on your rugged good looks.

Your eye contact, or lack thereof, can also be a huge issue with your leadership style. You need to be looking at your students, preferably in the eyes. Some people look at mouths instead of eyes. I am guilty of this bad habit, and it was not until recently that I found out why.

I tried to learn to play the piano at one time. My wife is an excellent pianist, and hearing her play made me want to have the same skill. Since I can tune a piano, I thought it might be a good idea to be able to play more than just one song. The only song I know is "Sweet Hour of Prayer," which always makes me look good after I finish tuning for someone.

I set out to learn piano only to discover that I could not see the treble and bass notes at the same time. I asked my wife about this and how she accomplished this feat. She told me that she sees both lines simultaneously. That clued me in on the fact that I was missing something that enabled me to see the notes. I later learned that I have a visual defect that was probably the cause of my difficulty reading in sixth and seventh grades. I later overcame the problem through an amazing remedial reading teacher.

In normal conversation, I look at a person's mouth instead of their eyes, and I now know why. I cannot see the mouth and eyes at the same time. Since the body part that conveys the most emotion is the mouth, I look at the mouth to accomplish this task. This practice is tied to self-esteem in all human beings.

This brings me back to my point. Any normal person without this visual defect can look at both the eyes and the mouth simultaneously. This story from my life taught me that eye contact is important for more than just the obvious reasons.

Many studies have shown that eye contact will increase retention. You will only retain a certain percentage of information that you hear. When you add a visual stimulus, that percentage goes up. When you combine the visual stimulus with an activity, you will have another leap in retention. Combine all of these techniques with an emotional stimulus, and you will have complete retention.

If you are anything like me in this area, you need to work constantly to keep your head up, making eye contact at all times. Encouraging students to look at you is a valuable aspect of this routine. By doing these two things, you exude confidence to your students and ensure they will hear what you say. This is yet another tool that puts you in charge of your class, enhancing others' perception of you as a leader.

Classroom Questions and Activities

1. Reflect on your current ability to use eye contact.

22
Routine #13: Let Us Pause for a Moment of Silence.

"Silence is a true friend that will never betray."
Confucius, 500 B.C.

Maintaining a quiet classroom is a necessary task for all educators. Noise distracts the learner from focusing on what you are saying and can be the main reason you cannot deliver your content in an efficient way. There are many ways of using silence to your advantage. This is necessary for good classroom management.

A few seconds of silence is powerful after you gain attention and stop distractions. It is not enough for you just to stand there and look mad, thinking that the students will somehow read your thoughts and have compassion on your miserable existence. You must communicate your intentions to them in varied ways, and you must maintain silence before you begin teaching.

When I first started teaching, I would stand there in my classroom looking out across a vast sea of students who were misbehaving. I would glare at them as if they would sense my anger toward their behavior. The frustration was obvious and showed itself through my body language and stiff demeanor. I would then blow up at them for not reading my mind.

It did not take me long to discover that my actions were giving control to the students. They could see that they had the upper hand and made use of this power to make sure that they retained their control of the classroom. I am sure that you can relate to this from your early career.

The silence I am showing you here is very different. You must realize that all your routines, when combined, will allow you to have the control that is necessary to make your use of

91

silence effective. Simply standing there without words will not be enough. Silence can only be accomplished in an effective way when you have a firm grip on the class and establish it in a calm and controlled manner.

By following these simple steps, you can focus attention your way. First, gain attention, and then pause without saying anything. Look around at each student. Your full attention must be on them for this to be effective. Correct additional problems verbally, and pause again. If you have 10 seconds of silence, you can be relatively assured that the class will remain quiet while you talk. This is especially powerful in a large group. Pause after redirecting behavior each time. Check for a calm environment by scanning the room.

Pause is important because it shows the students that you notice what is going on in the room. Make use of body language and looks to convey what you expect. Redirect eye contact to your direction at all times. If they are looking at you, they cannot do anything else.

My assistant director occasionally uses a very effective technique. He has what he calls "silent Wednesdays." He directs his entire rehearsal without saying anything, and the students are expected to do the same. All directions are given by body language or with the dry erase board.

This is a good team-building activity and develops self-control in the students. In an instrumental music class, this activity also allows for constant lip-to-mouthpiece rehearsal and reinforces the concept of watching the teacher for direction. Silent rehearsal also allows the students a chance to lead their actions without verbal feedback from the teacher.

Silence is a powerful tool and should be used at key points to direct attention. Pausing in the middle of a sentence wakes the listener up. Directing your eyes and body language to a student can be a powerful and persuasive action when accompanied by a pause in your speaking.

Being able to use the sound of silence can also make a point more dramatic. If you are appealing to emotion, the use of silence can cause the listener to reflect on what you have said and create a mood that would otherwise be lost with constant sound. It gives the listener a chance to feel what is heard and adds a powerful element to your speaking style.

Saying nothing at all is just as powerful as saying the right thing at the right time. In some situations, a pause in speaking helps the listener ponder what he will say in reply. It is the lull in the conversation that creates an opportunity for the listener to bring his unique perspective to the front of the conversation.

It is not enough simply to say nothing. You must learn to let your silence speak louder than your words. If you can learn to do this effectively, then the next step is to deliver your lesson. If you practice proper routines, you can be sure that silence will be maintained. In the next few chapters, you will learn a few routines that will assist you in maintaining silence for a productive classroom environment. The previous three routines (expectations, eye contact, and monitoring) are merely the foundation for making this happen.

23
Routine #14: On Task or Out of Control

Have you ever noticed how quickly an hour goes by when the students are thoroughly engaged in your lesson? There are days when your lesson is so stimulating and fun that time seems to slip by completely. I can remember this happening to me just a few days ago.

We had just finished our holiday concert, and the students were returning for the final two weeks of school before Christmas break. This is typically a time when I get new music in the folders and pass in the previous semester's materials. I decided to pass out our pop tune first. This particular piece of music was a medley of movie highlights with several current Top 40 hits. The students were thrilled, and our first rehearsal went by in a flash.

If only every day could be this stimulating. As an educator, I search for ideas to create a certain mood with my classes. Since music is naturally stimulating and enhances emotion, this job is fairly easy. The hard part comes weeks later when the music is thoroughly rehearsed, and boredom starts to set in.

Keeping young minds on task can be difficult. As teachers, we do not always have the most interesting content to deliver. Finding ways to keep material fresh and keeping students focused can be a daunting proposition. You will make your job much easier if you learn to do a few simple things that can make all the difference when keeping students on task. The following tactics will help you ensure that students are on task at all times.

Plan Ahead
The most important step you can take is to plan. Having a good plan before you step in front of your class with a new project is vitally important. Even if you are a veteran teacher and have taught the same way for years, having a well

thought-out plan can make your class much more interesting and fun. Having a clear focus on your long-range goals and executing a clear plan is necessary to give your students a sense of direction and anticipation for what might be next.

You must realize that students want to be busy. They want to have fun and have constructive activities to occupy their time in a meaningful way. I am amazed at how this works in my class.

There are occasions when our normal band class is interrupted by a different bell schedule. On these days, I sometimes give students the choice of watching a movie for twenty minutes or playing their instruments. They usually choose playing their instruments. If it is a choice between a fun activity or a fun and productive activity, the fun and productive activity will always win.

Keep All Students Focused and Active
There are times when you must focus on a few students in your classroom and not the entire group. When students need to be taught separately, no student should be off task for more than a few minutes to avoid boredom, misbehavior, and loss of learning opportunities. You should always assume that free time, even for a few of your students, will end up badly for you in the end. Most misbehavior originates from idle hands. "Idle hands are the devil's workshop"; they don't call this a truism for nothing.

It is interesting to see what happens with the students who fall behind on their instruments in my class. There are always a few students who fall behind in band because of a lack of talent or drive. When this occurs, the students will follow the same pattern each time. The progression is failure, lack of participation, boredom, and then misbehavior.

You should be able to see the same from your students when an activity is too difficult for one student while others are succeeding. To keep all students working when complex tasks are required, it may be necessary to give slower students only one task at a time, then adding additional tasks after momentum is gained. Some non-motivated students may have trouble getting started when there is a large multi-task project assigned. Giving a student a separate and easier task may start the student moving and will help you maintain better control in the end.

Use Emotion
Students will be most engaged in your class when you have a well thought-out plan that also taps into emotion. Some of the best preaching I have heard is done in this way. I have listened to many preachers, and the best ones always have a well-developed sermon that flows forward toward a point that taps into varied emotions. Many emotions can be used. Laughter, sadness, empathy, and compassion are just a few. Tapping into the emotions that make us human is critical if you plan to keep the attention of a young mind.

Avoid Free Time
You can bet that most of your discipline problems will occur when students are not focused on a task that you have selected. Boredom is the entire reason a non-motivated student misbehaves. Boredom can happen for many reasons and will always motivate a student to cause trouble and self-stimulate. I said before that students enjoy being busy and having their time occupied with meaningful activities. By allowing students free time, you invite them to find their own stimulating activities. These activities will always go against your plan for the class, so focusing activity toward your plan and keeping students occupied with meaningful activities should be your goal.

Create tasks for everyone, and never let a student or group of students question what they should be doing. By allowing students to have free time at the end of class, you can potentially waste weeks of your teaching time. A free day is the worst activity you can plan and only creates lost opportunities. Students do not earn lost opportunities, and by giving them something they cannot earn, you simply waste their time and yours.

Do you realize that if you waste five minutes a day of class just taking roll over 180 days, you waste fifteen hours of class? That is two weeks of content or rehearsal down the drain. Ouch! What if you waste ten or fifteen minutes a day? Add up all the meaningless time you waste in a day, and then ask yourself what opportunities you may have missed.

Ask yourself what your time means to you. When you get home on any given day, do you simply do nothing? If you are like me, you have a list of tasks, even fun activities to fill your time. Rarely do you ever just sit without doing something meaningful. Your students are counting on you to give meaning to their time. Do not let them down.

I hope that by this point, your perspective is changing. You now see how your teaching style can give meaning to your students' time. In the next few chapters, you will see how keeping students on task can be affected by other factors in your teaching style. Giving attention to a few minor details can give you giant leaps in the effectiveness of your overall delivery.

24
Routine #15: Don't Count Time, Make Time Count

"The superior man makes the difficulties he faces his first interest. Success will come later." Confucius, 500 B.C.

If you want to cover your material and make use of your time, then the pace of your teaching must be controlled to accommodate the unique needs of your students. To accomplish this, it will be necessary to give careful attention to the specific needs of your audience. Learning to control the pace of instruction will assist you in having a calm classroom and will maximize your use of the most precious resource you have—your time.

Think of it this way. When you are in church and you are listening to the preacher preach, what are your thoughts? Is the sermon unrelenting, just right, or unbelievably slow? Depending on your perspective as a church member, it could be any of these choices. Much of it depends on how quickly you want to eat lunch or how deeply the sermon touches your needs. Your perspective on the quality of the sermon is therefore related less to the preaching and more to other factors. It works this way for your students.

You will have a broad range of students in your classroom, and one teaching speed will not cover all students. For some gifted students, a fast-paced lesson for an hour may work well. Teaching at a fast pace may be fine for your gifted students since they are capable of processing the information.

For others, a slow pace may be the more appropriate choice. Many of the students that will attend your classes will have difficulty processing information with a fast-paced lesson. Many of the behavior problems you experience will be directly related to the speed at which you teach. Too fast, and you lose the slower students. Too slow, and you bore the gifted students. Finding the optimal pace is the key.

The needs of your audience should be carefully considered. Once you have a grip on this, you can develop your delivery style to suit their unique needs. Incorporating a varied method and teaching style suddenly becomes much easier to accomplish.

I have found this to be true in my own classes. Band is the kind of class that demands excellence from everyone. One rotten musician can spoil the whole bunch. As a director, I must ensure that everyone gets the music. I have noticed that it is easy to move too quickly through a rehearsal and lose the less talented musicians. Pace is important in this case, and it is my responsibility to ensure the success of everyone, no matter his or her learning style. If one student fails, the entire group could fail.

Your pace may be driven less by the students and more by your own sense of failure avoidance. How you see the overall picture is critical. You may be feeling pressure from your school district to get through as much of the required course material as possible. In doing this, you rush through your tasks without covering the material thoroughly. As a band director, I am not in a position to tell you how to approach this problem. I can only point out that you need to be aware of how this affects your pace.

There are times in my own situation when I feel similar pressure. I may be rehearsing a difficult piece of music with limited time before the performance. This is when that fear of failure creeps in and agitates my pace. In these times, I remember this truth: I will not see the big picture if all I look at are the mistakes that are made along the way.

I first listen to what the song sounds like overall. I get the big picture and then reduce the rehearsal down to the most difficult parts. If a particular section needs more attention, I work that section or assign students playing tests to encourage rehearsal at home. I constantly work on one problem at a time until I am only left with the easiest parts at the end. The easier parts normally work themselves out along the way, and we are left with a brilliant performance in the end. If you are careful along the way and use your time wisely, it is possible to accomplish this with time to spare.

Teaching pace can be a critical routine, even for a veteran teacher. Learning to pace your delivery can mean the difference between success and failure. Developing your teaching style will require your constant attention to this detail.

Classroom Questions and Activities

1. Write a few paragraphs describing a teacher from your past who had good or bad pace in his or her teaching style. How did this affect you as a student?

2. Rate your current teacher or professor for his or her pace in teaching. Do not hold back. Articulate what you really think. This is your big chance.

By this point, I feel that you and I are now friends. A good friend will go two miles when asked to go one. That's what friends do for each other. If you could just send one or two e-mails telling your other friends about my book, I would deeply appreciate your kindness. I'm touched to have such a kind friend.

25
Routine #16: Becoming a Supermodel

All teaching activities that you engage in should include thorough explanation and constant modeling practices. Modeling is simply showing something done right. As a teacher, you must model to teach. All teachers do this naturally, and it is not something you really need to be taught. You are constantly modeling whether you know it or not; but the question is, are you modeling effectively?

In my class, modeling may involve playing my trumpet with a good tone quality when talking about ways to produce a good sound or when demonstrating proper articulation. Modeling could be a simple hand gesture to show a student a fingering. Modeling may involve singing the part while the student struggles to hear the melody.

To model effectively, you should be creative. Make sure that what you do will assist the students in their overall understanding. It is possible to model in a negative or dull manner. Much of your expertise in modeling will come from other abilities that you develop along the way as an effective leader. Developing skills that contribute to effective modeling will be essential to your success.

When I first started teaching beginners to play their instruments, I realized that trombone and tuba players had a hard time hearing their parts. I needed a skill to assist them besides my voice. I picked up a bass guitar and taught myself how to play their parts. This gave me a new tool to assist my modeling skills and proved to be just what they needed to progress at a faster pace.

For large groups, modeling and pace must both be considered together. For instance, if you model how to cross the break on a clarinet in a band class for 20 minutes and forget about keeping the drummers busy, you run the risk of your band room being burned to the ground. (Don't ever leave the drummers alone with any time on their hands.)

Keep everyone focused on what you are doing when you model. You will avoid breakdowns in your routine by doing this. You can now see that modeling, pacing, and keeping students on task are all routines that are interconnected. Knowing this fact can be the difference between getting through your textbook in a year and being stuck and bogged down by your lack of efficient delivery.

No matter how good you are, there are teachers out there who can outperform you in the classroom when it comes to presenting material. What you might not realize is this: You can learn the same techniques and be that teacher yourself. Achieving this may involve learning new talents, so don't be afraid to be creative.

In addition to modeling your content, you must consider how students see you as their model for behavior. Students will learn to model your behavior and attitudes. Your behavior and character may be the key element in the emotional growth of your students. It is not enough to teach them your lesson. You must teach them how to live, how to care, how to show compassion, and how to be a seeker of knowledge. Being passionate about your area of expertise is important, but modeling good character gives the students a reason to believe in what you say. If you have poor judgment and faulty character, no one will care what you have to say.

Keeping students on task, pacing your instruction, and modeling are all interrelated ideas. Each of these routines can complement the others if executed properly. Having a clear plan that is focused around these routines will ensure your overall success and minimize the possibility of misbehavior from your students.

Classroom Questions and Activities

1. Create at least one unique modeling activity and demonstrate it for the class in the form of a lesson. Compete with your classmates for the most ingenious idea. Read the next chapter to get ideas for incorporating technology into your presentation. Remember to model what you teach.

26
Routine #17: Where's the Any Key?

Technology can be your friend. Learn to use it well, and make it part of your teaching style whenever possible. I realize that some educators are afraid of technology. Gadgets can be intimidating to an educator who has been in the classroom since the dawn of history. Learning to use technology in this case may take some time. If you are in this situation, ask a younger teacher or relative to give you lessons. Seek help, and don't be so set in your ways that you are afraid to try something new.

Our choir director in our high school was in this situation when she moved from the intermediate school a few years ago. We share the music room, and I had recently added several pieces of audio and video technology to the front of the classroom. It took some time for her to adapt to the new equipment.

Once she got some momentum, she started purchasing her own equipment. She added a hand-held recorder, which she used to record her rehearsals. She also added a wireless microphone to the sound system so her students could better hear her. She eventually moved her entire music library and her classroom information to an online management system. It only took a willingness to learn and a realization that technology could enhance her teaching.

One more helpful technique is to have directions for each device printed and placed somewhere near the device. This will assist you in making the equipment work when you need it. Be creative, and you will soon be gaining the edge that technology can provide.

It is obvious that technology can be helpful, but technology can also cost you your job if you are not careful. The internet is filled with useful information but it is also inundated with some of the most harmful and vulgar depictions that can be witnessed by your students. Monitoring the use of technology is critical if you want to keep your job. It can be easy to bring an unexpected image or sound to your students' attention, so careful prescreening of material is necessary. Be on guard with technology, and avoid unexpected surprises.

Using technology saves time and can be another tool for moving a class forward. It motivates and excites students and can aid in aiming your students' focus up front. Students are visual learners, so using a variety of techniques to illustrate your lesson will increase the odds that they pick up the information that you are trying to convey. As an added benefit, technology will make teaching more interesting for you.

Classroom Questions and Activities

1. Place yourself within the walls of your new classroom. Create a technology wish list. Research the cost of each item and create a purchase order. Share with the class.

27
Routine #18: The Greatest Gift That Life Can Grant Us

"Surprise is the greatest gift that life can grant us." This quote from Boris Pasternak, a Nobel-prize winning poet from Russia, is a fitting reminder that surprise can be a powerful tool when added to your teaching routine. As discussed earlier, you should always teach in unexpected ways and with varied methods. Expectations for behavior should be the only routine aspect of your classroom.

There are several ways that surprise can enhance your routines. Listen to a good comedian. It's not always what they say that is so funny but the delivery that leads to the laugh. That is why you can tell a joke that you heard and nobody laughs. Delivery is important in humor, and surprise is the gift that keeps on giving.

Earlier in this book, you heard me rattling off some deep sentence only to insert an unexpected word like peanut butter or butter instead of better. That's funny because you didn't expect a serious book to be unexpectedly silly. Don't be afraid to throw some surprise into your teaching from time to time.

I try to use humor in my classroom whenever possible. One of my most memorable experiences with this was when we were on our final rehearsal for a big competition in Chicago. We were leaving for the eight-hour trip in three days and were wrapping up on the last practice. Everyone was very serious, and we had accomplished all we could. The students were tired.

My assistant director was on the podium trying to rehearse the last note of the piece, and he kept having the kids play the note with more energy. I was standing right behind him, and each time he had them play the note, I would act as if I were stripping off part of my outer shirt. There was actually a reason for this.

We hid our new Chicago shirt from the students and were just about to reveal the design for the first time. I picked this time to start the process of letting them see the back of the new shirt. They laughed hard each time I pulled off a piece of my outer shirt. The assistant director went with it and kept them playing the note again until I finally had the outer shirt completely off. Kids were crying they were laughing so hard. My assistant director took off his outer shirt, and we both turned to reveal the Chicago shirt.

The big surprise on the back of the shirt was a digital rendering of me and my assistant director looking like blue men from the Blue Man Group, complete with bald heads. When I finally turned and showed them the shirt, they were completely surprised and excited. That is a moment I will never forget, and I am sure they will never forget either. Surprise is an amazingly powerful emotion when combined with other positive emotions like humor.

We competed in the competition the next week and won first place in our class and first place overall with the highest score of the day. We competed against 25 bands from all around the Midwest, and the excitement generated from this success is still with us to this day. Our next big trip is to Disney World, and the students could not be more excited.

Classroom Questions and Activities

1. Develop a lesson idea that starts with surprise. Share with the class. The greatest surprise wins.

28
Routine #19: If You Can't Take the Heat, Don't Tickle the Dragon

Use humor with extreme caution and care. Everyone loves humor. Laughter is an important motivator that builds a bond with the teacher. If you are not careful, though, humor can lead to a meltdown in your routine. Maintain your routines at all costs, even when you make students laugh. If you use humor, prepare to accept what happens, and be ready to bring them back to your ideal behavior after the laughing has stopped.

Be sure to watch for abrupt commentary from the students when this happens. They will always want to interject something funny themselves. Make sure they raise a hand to speak, and don't let them blurt out. Once you have made them laugh, keep them controlled.

In this book, you have heard me use a few lame attempts at humor. I have done this to illustrate the importance of humor to your leadership style. If you are going to be a charismatic leader, you cannot be stiff. Kids do not associate well with a stiff leadership style.

Your use of humor can equalize your need for control against their need for constant stimulation. Humor can bring their attention to you and make them hear what you are saying. It can increase the pace of your class and add surprise to your delivery. Using humor in a controlled manner will enhance your routines. Go ahead and tickle the dragon occasionally, but be ready to deal with the flames.

One part of my life that I really enjoy is my satellite radio. I love to listen to a good comedian deliver his material. I am constantly looking for new ideas to use in my classroom. Using a story to illustrate a point is powerful, and when the story contains humor, the point can come alive.

Listen to a good comedian sometime and learn his delivery method. Try it out in your classroom and see what happens. You may crash and burn, but even that can be very entertaining. Remember to be careful with your humor, and keep it appropriate. If you tickle your kids too hard, you might get burned.

Classroom Questions and Activities

1.   Create a lesson plan that includes humor. Share the lesson with the class, and use your classroom management skills to control the behavior of the class as you teach. Three students should be selected as class clowns. All students should be encouraged to contribute freely according to their own personalities.

29
Routine #20: The Principal is Not Your Pal

Never make your lack of classroom management the principal's job. Do your job first and exhaust all options before you ever contact the office. The principal just might appreciate it and give you a new smart board. You never know.

I have had many interesting principals over the years. They have each had unique styles and approaches for dealing with discipline and motivation. I will relate a few stories from my experiences with these principals in the remainder of this chapter.

My second job as an educator was in southeast Missouri. One of the many lessons I learned from this job was that the authorities above me were wise and had experiences that could help me develop my teaching style. I realize that now, but at the time, I was rebellious to their corrections and suggestions. My ego kept me from seeing their wisdom. They were the old guys, and I was the sharp, young, and intelligent new teacher with the enthusiasm to make things happen. As it turns out, I was wrong.

I assumed that the principal was sitting in his office waiting for the next student that I would send down. As far as I knew, this was his only job. College had not taught me that the principal had other duties besides discipline. Now, after years of having to learn from my mistakes, I see how wrong I was.

One of the principals in this district, the assistant principal, had a very calm and quiet persona. He was a real yes man and told me everything I wanted to hear. I liked him, but I didn't really learn much from him other than how to be a nice guy.

The other principal was more of a walking ego. He had charisma, but he was very much like what I would imagine Caesar to be. He even looked like him. He looked just like Roosevelt on the dime. He would look at me through my classroom door and stare as if I were doing something wrong. I probably was and didn't realize it, or worse, someone was probably goofing off or smoking something in the back of the room that I didn't see.

I would send my misbehaving students down to his office in a single file line to get their paddling. I will never forget how he did this. He would tell the student to bend over his desk and look at the open barn door of the painting on the wall. He told the students to look for the horse in the barn. I tried to look each time, and I never did see that horse.

Eventually, sometime around second quarter, he told me that I should possibly start looking at ways to take care of my classroom problems on my own. He didn't exactly use those words, however. I think it was more like, "Can't you do anything right? These kids are walking all over you, and you're making me do all your dirty work."

I resented him for years. Some of the comments he made about my teaching and my constant discipline problems aggravated me at that time. I saw much success from my students in the three years I was there, and all he could do was look like the bitter beer guy and make snide remarks. After a few years and a new school district, his concerns for my educational method started making sense to me and echoed in my head each time I encountered the same problems.

Long after I had left that school district, I would draw from his words. He was right, and I knew it. I now see him for what he really was. He was an effective principal who wasn't afraid to push my buttons a little to get me moving. I can't say that I agreed with his delivery, but his words were invaluable to my future as an educator.

This school really had its issues. There was racial division all across the school and community. Discipline was strict and needed to be. In the short time that I was there, I witnessed drug abuse, violence in the classroom, abuse from the home, the aftereffects of rape, and constant fighting among the students. This experience gave me skill in dealing with discipline issues and allowed me to gain self-confidence when dealing with harsh behavior. I was green in my first year but sharp as a tack when I left.

The school district that I worked in one year before this gave me a different picture entirely when it came to principals and student behavior. This principal was old, stern, and set in his ways. Although respected for good management, there were occasional grumblings from the staff. His style of leadership was harsh but also gave me a wake-up call in certain areas.

I only taught in this school for one semester. I had graduated college in December, and this school happened to have an opening at that time. I rented a house from the superintendent and lived right next door to him. This school was in a small town, and I had very few discipline problems there. The students were well adjusted in this small community, and they loved their teachers.

One of the valuable lessons that I learned in this job was that I would be very poor if I did not do something to supplement my income. I had not yet married my fiancée, and I was barely making it on my $21,200 salary. At the end of each month, I was eating canned ravioli and chips. My school lunch was the best meal of the day.

Fortunately, my father had taught me to tune pianos. This turned out to be the skill that kept me from going broke each month. I charged $40 for each piano tuning. This was enough to let me go to the city (6,000 residents) and get some real food. My nuggets never tasted better.

A few years later, my wife and I decided to move to Illinois near her family. The school district there was a small Community Unit district containing all classes K-12 in one building. Our superintendent was calm and had a very witty sense of humor. He also served as our principal and was another unique leader.

This principal was very approachable and willing to listen. His advice was very solid, and he could lead with a calm and assertive attitude. This was a healthy influence in my early career. His friendly and helpful attitude was a refreshing change.

The elementary principal in this district was the former football coach. The stadium carried his name, and he was an icon in the community. He was overly friendly and used every opportunity to find aspects of my teaching style that were worthy of praise. He appreciated my hard work and took opportunities to notice my dedication.

I had never met an administrator who was as free with compliments as this principal. When he passed out our paychecks, he required us to shake his hand before he would hand the goods over to us. He found something nice to say that showed we had earned our pay.

I spent eight good years in this school and saw my first fifth-grade beginning band through to their senior year. I had many wonderful experiences in this district and built the band program to its height. Illinois classified us as 2A, and my high school band program had ninety members when I left the district. We won many awards and traveled across the Midwest on four band tours.

My band grew so large in the junior high that the district rescheduled the entire seventh hour. The only teachers who didn't have their planning time that hour were the drama teacher and art teacher, and they were not happy with me for this. I didn't just have the good students, I had all the students. Those were good days for me, and my leadership style was beginning to develop momentum.

I now teach in a school district in Missouri. My current principals are the most professional leaders I have had. I am not just saying that because they may read this book. Building a strong educational community is their main commitment. Our administration has completely turned over in the last few years, and we now have new superintendents and principals leading the way. The future continues to look bright.

I could not have found a better school district to work in, and it is mainly due to a mix of committed educators and administrators. Our motto is "Where Kids are First!" That one statement speaks volumes about our district. I have a great deal of pride toward my current school district, as do all the teachers. We share a common vision, and success is all around us.

I have worked hard over the last seven years to draw from my experience and developed a unique and effective leadership style. Being part of an energetic educational atmosphere, as we have in our district, allows me the freedom to make this a reality. It is entirely possible for you to experience the same joy in teaching that I experience every day. Believe in yourself first, and the rest will follow.

It is vital for you to build good relationships with your administration. Constantly using them as your tool for discipline will only harm this relationship. Learning from them as examples, good or bad, to improve your own leadership style is the key. Draw on them for support but do not make them your mommies. A good principal or administrator will be able to do his job much more effectively if you do yours.

Classroom Questions and Activities

1. Describe your favorite or least favorite principal.

The following page contains a list of all routines in a concise format. **Feel free to make photocopies** of this page for you and your colleagues as long as the title is preserved. Enlarge this page 129% to get a full-page view. Read it each day before you enter the classroom as a reminder of good classroom management.

Classroom Management Routines
From the book,

The Superior Educator

A Calm and Assertive Approach
to Classroom Management
and Large Group Motivation

By *Stephen T. McClard*

www.SuperiorEd.com

- Maintain a Healthy Diet
- Get Plenty of Sleep
- Envision the Ideal
- Be Organized
- Follow Rules Consistently/ Strategically Enforce
- Gain Attention
- Stop Distractions Before Teaching
- Hunt for Abrupt Verbal Commentary
- Redirect Behavior Constantly
- Communicate Expectations
- Monitor Your Environment
- Make and Demand Eye Contact
- Use Silence to Your Advantage
- Stay on Task
- Consider Time Management and Pace
- Model and Demonstrate Regularly
- Use Technology
- Use Surprise
- Use Humor with Caution
- Avoid "Using" the Principal

30
Large-Group Motivation – Dealing With Fear

Motivating a large group will involve developing consistent routines and a healthy bit of charisma. Charisma is a subject covered in the next chapter. As you read this chapter, be thinking about what your definition of charisma is and how your leadership style can influence the motivation of a large group.

By the end of this book, you should understand the basic tools you will need to be successful in large-group settings and feel confident the next time you face being "the one" in a large crowd. Combined with the routines listed above, these ideas will assist you in developing your own unique charismatic leadership style. Even if you never step into a leadership position for a large group, you can still gain many advantages by preparing yourself to do so.

Having the confidence and charisma to gain these skills will first involve overcoming fear. "Enochlophobia" is the fear of large crowds. We all suffer from this fear at one point or another. Education professionals like band directors, coaches, and principals will typically have this fear in check on a daily basis. The fears associated with managing a crowd can be conquered by understanding the dynamics of a large group of students and the inner workings of your own unique personality.

The first and most important fear that you will experience is a genuine feeling of inadequacy. This fear is the main cause of all anxieties that you experience in the classroom. You might say, "I'm only one person. How will I deal with this large group?"

This is the thought that should continually run through your mind: you will perform to your own expectations. Remember, you can go as far as your mind lets you. Self-imposed limitations will create obstacles not your students.

Most people only achieve to a fraction of their capacity, so you need to decide what it is about your unique personality that keeps you from achieving at a high level.

Self-esteem is the key piece of the puzzle when dealing with these fears and is the tool that you need to be successful in a large-group setting. Experience gained through being successful in stressful situations will improve your self-esteem. The more you have experiences that try your skills, the more you will learn about controlling your actions and thereby improving your self-esteem. Confidence and the feeling of being self-assured will not come overnight. You have heard it before that "admitting you have a problem is the first step to overcoming a problem."

Fear of failure is another overwhelming source of anxiety in dealing with large groups. This is the constant nagging belief that your actions might cause others to see you as inadequate or cause your group to fail. Succumbing to this fear ultimately becomes a self-fulfilling prophecy. By seeing yourself in the light of inadequacy, you therefore exude this to the people around you and diminish their optimism.

Fear is the one emotion that can incapacitate you as a leader and make you instantly unsuccessful. Your audience will see this in just a few seconds of meeting you for the first time. When you give in to these fears, you hand over control to your audience.

The trick is to discover how to take charge from the first moment and set your foot down as a confident leader. You must be able to achieve this without being obvious that you are trying to do so. In this book, I can only share what you need to do with the fear factor. The rest is up to you. Believe in yourself first, and the rest will follow.

As you can see so far, leading a large group starts with self-confidence. We will now look at a few confidence-building ideas, which will ultimately lead you to the main personality trait you need as a successful large-group leader: the persona of charisma.

Classroom Questions and Activities

1. What fears do you have when dealing with large groups? Give a few examples.

31
Developing Charisma

Charisma is that magic quality you have seen in people who make you instantly like them. You may not even be able to put your finger on just what it is about the person that makes you feel this way. This leadership style is magnetic, and it drives the desire in others to produce results. Charisma is elusive at best, and developing charisma involves much more than what I discuss here. Developing this trait is an individual endeavor, and I can only allude to its significance in your leadership style.

Charisma is not a quality that everyone will see in you, and it may not even be a quality that is readily seen within your current personality. One person may feel this about you while another person sees no charisma at all. Developing charisma that gains attention from more than just a few select people is a difficult proposition. Despite this, it is possible to exude charisma to a large group that sees you each day and knows you by your leadership style. Many people refer to this as developing respect. If respect is what you earn, then developing charisma and solid leadership is how you get there.

Building charisma starts with self-confidence. You must have some form of an ego to lead with charisma. My sister told me, after reading this, that she now knows why all the band directors at the state convention act so self-confident. If you cannot be self-confident, you cannot continue to the next steps of developing a charismatic leadership style. Working with large groups of students will be very difficult without moving past this point.

Have you ever noticed how fast you can complete a complex task when you are highly motivated to do so? When you are not motivated, a simple task like mowing the lawn can take days to get started. How fast does your lawn get done when company is coming over? What changed your energy level? Could it possibly be that you were trying to impress them?

The success you experience in dealing with large groups is directly proportional to the energy you put into your leadership toward the goals that you set for your group. Notice that I did not say the energy you "feel" toward your goals. The way you feel about putting energy and effort toward an important task should be meaningless without something motivating you first. It is all about the willingness to put effort into the task and the driving force behind this willingness that matters.

All your strategies, beliefs, routines, optimism, and intellect will be useless without the energy and drive to accomplish a goal. Actively building and utilizing energy toward momentum is the first step to building charisma. Give yourself reasons to succeed, and the energy will follow. Building energy toward success and going against your fear will build confidence. Building confidence, one success at a time, will continually develop the foundation for a charismatic leadership style.

The second step to building your confidence and developing charisma is your willingness to improve mental mediation. When you mediate, you find alternative resolutions to your mental conflicts. Cognitive dissonance constantly bombards our thinking. This mental conflict is defined as two separate and conflicting beliefs about one thing. Your ability to deal with cognitive dissonance is paramount to mediating your decisions. Quickly mediating your inner conflicts, therefore, aids in your ability to exude confidence and relax your overall demeanor.

Earlier in this book, I mentioned a story about a student who set fire to my band room carpet. The instant this happened, I immediately broke into action. I rushed to the scene, moved students into the hall, and had the fire alarm pulled. Quick action on my part illustrates my point. For more ideas and insight into mental mediation, read the book *Blink* by

Malcolm Gladwell. His book describes the decisions we make in the first few instances of any situation.

When you can successfully mediate your inner thoughts, you will appear more relaxed. You will look confident and suddenly see others as your equals. You will no longer have the constant feeling of inadequacy. Others will look to you for leadership and solid judgment.

When you consider your skills as a confident group leader, you must be aware of a few important ideas. Eye contact and holding your head up is an essential skill for a confident and charismatic leader. By holding your head high, you show your level of pride in yourself. Controlling your eye contact is necessary if you want to read people properly and exude confidence. Eye contact is difficult for some people to maintain but is a necessary step in developing charisma. It shows your audience that you have a high degree of self-esteem. Keep your head up, and look proud if you expect anyone to take you seriously.

Another step in the development of charisma and confidence involves your emotional control. You must be able to restrain and express emotion simultaneously. This must be done in a calm and assertive manner. Being calm and assertive, as discussed earlier, will assist you in showing genuine emotion with amazing optimism and will enhance others' perception of you as a charismatic leader.

The attributes that make us human are always visible in strong leaders. Warmth, compassion, and understanding are just a few. If these emotions are missing in your leadership style, you will be seen as harsh and unfeeling. Negative and fearful emotions are dangerous when worn on the sleeve. Controlling the expression of these emotions, however, is a significant consideration for building charisma and being confident. The ability to control negative emotion is different for each personality type, so you will need to examine your own personality to see how much work needs to be done to keep your emotional restraint intact.

You need to consider carefully how powerful your charisma can be to a young child. It is easy to be so convincing to a young mind that you actually instill too much serious emotion into an activity and cause constant fear in the student. Girls are especially vulnerable to these emotions. If you are not careful, tears will flow. A well-motivated student can hit the end of their world if they think you are disappointed in them. You must make them know you care.

This next step is vitally important and something that we can all learn to eventually do; that is to think before we speak. How many times have you blurted out something without considering your audience? Being a credible leader involves being truthful and watchful of every word; not that any of the idiots reading this book would really care. Misspeaking or speaking out of anger is one of the quickest ways to kill your charisma as I just did in the sentence above. Notice the feeling you had when you read that I thought of you as an idiot. Expressing these negative thoughts will destroy your confidence and harm the perception that others have of your leadership. If your negative language is overheard, you may unwittingly damage your credibility.

"The superior man puts actions before words. Afterwards, he speaks according to his actions." Confucius, 500 B.C.

Being confident will demand that you do not say words that you will feel guilty for later. When you think something negative about someone, you should keep it inside. If you are honest, positive, and truthful all the time with your tongue, you never need to remember what you said, just that you spoke from your convictions in an honest manner. Eliminate the guilt by knowing that you are always speaking with consideration to others. You remember what Grandma always said, "If you don't have anything good to say, don't say anything at all."

"The man who speaks without modesty will find it difficult to make his words pleasing to others." Confucius, 500 B.C.

I'll never forget something that happened to me at my first job. I had not been teaching for more than a few months when I was working with high school drummers on a difficult rhythm. I was standing in the back of the room with them, right next to a short and sassy little freshman who was acting like a wise guy. Not only was he acting goofy, but he also couldn't play what I was asking him to play. In retrospect, he really wasn't being all that bad. My perception of the situation was most likely skewed by my stress level.

To make matters worse, I hadn't had much sleep, and I was anxious about an upcoming performance that the principal, in his infinite wisdom, had thrown on us because he didn't think we were busy enough. It was also right before contest, so I was very resentful that we were asked to give a "Pop" concert at that time of year.

The drummer in question had pushed one too many of my buttons, and the next thing I knew, I said, "NO! What's wrong with you that you can't get this right? It's so easy a sixth grader could do it!" That's not the worst of it. In my anger, I thumped him on the chest with my drumstick before I could think. I didn't do it hard, but I did it nonetheless. This was not one of my more shining moments.

I really felt bad about it. I was embarrassed that I had let my emotions get the best of me. I was young and had much to learn about dealing with these emotions. College had not educated me in these life lessons. I did not fully understand that thumping a student with a drumstick would be any different than using the paddle, which we could still do at that time. I always had the art teacher next door paddle for me. She had an amazing swing.

The next day, I brought the student in and apologized. I told him that I was under a great deal of stress. I made sure he knew that I was out of line for making him look bad in front of the other kids and that I should not have lost control the way I did.

It turned out that he was a good listener and related to my feelings with a story of his own about the problems he was having with his family situation. He told me something that I will never forget or get tired of hearing from my students. He said, "It's okay, Mr. McClard. I love band, and you're still my favorite teacher." I could hardly keep from tearing up when I heard those words come out of his mouth. He is about the only student that I can remember well from that school.

In the end, we were both better for what had happened and became better connected as the year progressed. The concert, on the other hand, was painful to hear. That is, except for one spot where the little drummer played his part perfectly and then looked at me with a thumbs-up and a wink after the song was over. I learned many lessons that year about keeping my emotions and words under control.

Another part of controlling your tongue involves how you speak. If making good habits as a leader is the goal, then breaking bad habits must also be the goal. Avoid using "okay," "um," "ah," and "er" when addressing students or large crowds. We all have these types of habits when communicating. Speaking this way makes us appear unintelligent and unrefined. Charisma will demand that we communicate well with people and choose our words with care.

Having your body language under control is also an important communication tool when building charisma. Matching your body language to your words and emotions is incredibly significant to building charisma. A charismatic leader will do this in a skillful way. We can examine a figure from history to see how body language plays into charisma.

I hesitate to use Adolph Hitler as a role model here, but his use of body language speaks volumes about his ability to control the minds of people. Hitler was undoubtedly a charismatic figure to the citizens of Germany. His mastery of body language allowed him to control and manipulate an entire country and was directly tied to his ability to control his energy, confidence, emotions, and words. Unfortunately for the world, his charisma was used in a shockingly evil manner but points to its awesome power.

Hitler's ability to be a charismatic figure should clearly demonstrate the power of body language in building charisma. Despite these amazing abilities, it is interesting how charismatic actions do not always end well. It is possible to be charismatic and lead your group to failure. If careless, the choices you make along the way can undermine all your leadership skills. Charisma will then be seen as fake enthusiasm.

Have you ever noticed that you can instantly spot a person who has charisma? There is something magnetic about a person who has mastered these traits. The problem is this: charisma is not instantly gained. Certain qualities are necessary to be a successful charismatic leader, and not everyone can attain this magnetic personality right away.

As mentioned earlier, mediating your thoughts is a key to acting quickly and making good decisions. Being indecisive can bring a large group to a stand still. Your greatest enemy as a group leader is inactivity within the group. By taking action, you can change circumstances. By improving circumstances and pushing a group to success, you earn respect from the group and gain confidence in yourself. Each additional success adds to their respect of you and the respect you have for yourself.

A charismatic leader will always look at failure as an opportunity to learn instead of an excuse to quit. If you do not reach the results you want, don't take it personally. Instead, take it as a chance to grow. You should see that the important quality of a charismatic leadership style is a confident, tenacious persistence and drive for success balanced by a calm and assertive leadership style with the ability to make strong decisions that bring your group to success.

Ask yourself these questions when presented with failure:

- What mistakes were made?
- Why did these mistakes happen?
- How can I prevent it from happening again?
- When can I see this failure turned into a success?

Here is an example of how these questions were answered with a student that I had in my seventh-grade band a few years ago. It was my first year at the school, and I noticed that Tyler didn't have much success with his instrument. On many occasions, I would look back and find him asleep, slumped over his trombone. I knew his family life was solid and he was a good kid. I wasn't entirely sure why he was so bored with band. It was obvious that he was not thriving in my class.

As the next year went by, I tried everything I could to get him interested in being a better trombone player. Nothing worked. Eighth grade went by, and I somehow managed to keep Tyler in band for one more year. He had made some progress on his trombone, but I could still tell that he was bored to tears. The one thing that I could use to keep him in band his first year was the fact that we had a new jazz band in the schedule, and he was just beginning to play bass guitar in his spare time. I invited him to play trombone in the group and possibly bass guitar if he learned to read the music first. That's all it took. As I later found out, the instrument was the problem all along.

First semester in jazz band went well, but I could tell Tyler was still not completely happy. The same old problems were creeping back. I asked him to play one song with his bass. He played bass for me for the next three years and became an incredible musician. He would practice for hours, and his parents invested in a double bass that he also used in concert band. He started playing in church and formed his own jazz combo that performed around town.

Before he graduated, he received a full music scholarship to a Baptist college in Arkansas. Tyler is one of the most amazing musicians I have ever graduated from my program. Music became his passion in life.

Stories like these will make your job as a teacher worth all the work and will eventually assist you in developing your charismatic leadership style. It will not come overnight. You will build this over time and gain confidence through the feelings of success you instill in others.

Classroom Questions and Activities

1.   Do you consider yourself a charismatic personality? Explain.

2.   Describe at least one charismatic leader that you have known personally. What was it about him or her that revealed this persona?

32
Having a Clear Purpose

"If you think in terms of a year, you should plant a seed. If you think in terms of ten years, you should plant a tree. If you think in terms of 100 years, you should teach."
Confucius, 500 B.C.

In the previous chapter, you discovered a few ideas about building confidence and developing charisma. In the remaining chapters, you will see how you can take that confidence and charisma and turn them into results. The first step to seeing results brings us back to the first chapter— developing a vision.

Your vision is the paint for the canvas of expectations. Developing purpose determines how you will get where you want to go and inspires your decisions from that point on. Purpose gives the reason. Because of this, your students need to know the answer to the following question. Why are we doing this activity, and why will it benefit me personally?

Nothing is more frustrating than being part of an organization that has no clear purpose. As a calm, assertive, and charismatic leader, you have the obligation to bring purpose to every experience in a sequenced manner and make your followers believe in what they are doing. Successful large-group leadership depends on this clear and measured purpose. You can get people to do anything if they believe there is a purpose that will benefit them personally. The more you can sell this, the better group leader you will become and the more your group will achieve.

For me, the purpose I preach in my group is success in life and enjoyment of a skill that will enhance every aspect of life. Being a band member is one of the best success-building activities in a school district. This belief drives my passion for the work I do. If you are passionate about your program and what you are teaching, it will be evident to the students you teach.

A good way to reflect on your own personal convictions and overall purpose is to write down your philosophy of education. Your personal philosophy is the entire reason you became a teacher. If you do not have a vision and passion for what you do, developing a clear philosophy will be impossible.

Keep in mind that your philosophy will change over time. Writing your philosophy now will assist you in developing a deeper philosophy as your experience expands. Revise your philosophy often.

Here is my philosophy for music education:

Philosophy of Education
Stephen T. McClard

The following philosophy of music education is my opinion based on cumulative observations made from my career as a music educator. It is my belief that music education is an indispensable, developmental element of learning and should be taught throughout the life of a learner. It is also my contention that music education is a model of learning that should be studied and adapted by the educational community for its value as a cooperative learning and performance-based model.

The obvious benefits of music education are seen in the aesthetical growth that comes from appreciating and participating in the arts. As a student, performer, teacher, and luthier (stringed instrument builder), I know the impact that music has had in my own life, and I see its impact on each of the lives that it touches in my classroom. Music has an amazing ability to inspire thought and touch the soul, character, and desires of the mind in a manner that no other educational discipline can achieve.

More significantly, music education is an important vehicle by which a student develops and rehearses skills that are then carried forward to other disciplines. There is no other educational discipline that exists that draws from so many areas of learning in such a meaningful and fulfilling way. Certain cognitive thinking, problem solving, and higher order thinking skills that are needed for math, science, and reading are a natural byproduct of music training and, therefore, rehearsing these skills is indispensable for a well-rounded learner's development.

Lastly, music education is a time-honored practice that has not changed much over the last 1,000 years. Music style, music quality, and the technology of music have changed, but the basic technique of presenting information and then "using what you know" has not changed. Music education is the ultimate performance-based learning model, and music students are the ultimate learning community. Music education is a cooperative learning activity that never gets old and provides unquenchable variety and potential. Plato said it best with these words: "Music has the power to adjust and channel the collective consciousness of massive groups of people."

It is therefore my educational philosophy that, because of these advantages, music education is the best basic starting point for developing and equipping young minds to rehearse and apply a wide range of necessary thinking skills critical to every other educational endeavor.

Classroom Questions and Activities
1. Develop your own philosophy of education. Share with the class.

33
Building a Team

This chapter will highlight a few extra ideas that will help you be a successful group leader and classroom teacher. They are beneficial to building your class or program into a team and are necessary to enhance success. **It is rewarding to build your team yourself, but when the students build the team for you, everyone involved will experience the greatest success possible.**

Paying Attention to Detail

Attention to detail can mean the difference between success and mediocrity. Remember that a whole lot of small stuff creates the larger picture. The difference between winning and losing is always found in the least noticed details. When marching bands lose at marching events, it always comes down to a few points. I often wonder what one more point worth of effort would have required. Anyone can be good, but very few have the capacity to be great.

My personal technique for rehearsing bands is to work through the most obvious performance mistakes and then carefully work down to the most miniscule details. If I give up on the first reading of a piece of music, then I will never get to the final performance. I must first ignore the horrible sound and get on with the job of fixing all of the missed notes, key signatures, and wrong rhythms. It is the small details and varied problems that I must fix to get that perfect performance in the end.

The stronger I build the foundation from the beginning, the fewer mistakes I have to deal with along the way. Ideally, if I do my job in the early stages of developing a musician, the job of fixing key signatures, missed notes, and wrong rhythms is minimized. Start with a good foundation, and then work the details from large to small.

Another way to pay attention to detail is to keep lists. As a large-group leader, you have too many things going on to just simply remember what you need to do. Write your tasks down or keep them in an organizer. Set alarms and make sure you never miss any detail or appointment. When you see a task that needs to be done, do it immediately and then move on to the next item. Always stay one step ahead of your agenda.

Learning to Delegate

There really is no excuse not to delegate tasks. Assume that your students love to be busy and want to be helpful. When you ask students to do something for you, they generally feel better toward you after the task is complete. In the end, asking someone to help makes a short-term investment into a long-term payoff for your program. Avoid telling someone what to do. Ask and you shall receive.

A good example of this is with my son Andrew. I recently had a new student move into the district who played violin. This is not an instrument that we use in our band, so I told the student that we would help him learn a new instrument.

He showed up the next day with a trumpet and looked eager to get started. Since my assistant and I were busy teaching class, I asked my son to give the new trumpet player a few lessons in another room. My son did his job, and before long, he had taught the new student the basics of playing trumpet. He did this with no help from the assistant director or me. Our new trumpet player is now progressing through his beginning band book and has joined the band for the Christmas concert after only three weeks of practice. If I had not delegated this duty, the new student would not have made it past the first week of band without feeling lost and miserable.

By asking a student to do a task, you are really telling them that you value their experience and abilities. You move their value into the program and make them realize that without their help, you would be unable to proceed. By trusting a student to help, you gain a capable and willing leader. The next time you need something done, take the opportunity to enhance a student's self-esteem.

Many students have a constant feeling of worthlessness. If there is a task they can perform for you that will make them a success, if even for a moment, you have forever changed a life. Your trust and admiration can be a life-changing feeling. The more you can foster this feeling in your students, the more your students will buy into your group and see you through the eyes of respect.

One way that I delegate in my marching band is to create a student leadership duty sheet. I assign all sections specific jobs that must be done at each home game. They range from supervision of the trailer loading to cleaning up after the game is over. Every conceivable task is covered. At the end of the night, I always compliment students for their amazing work. Jobs are efficiently accomplished, and there is less worry for me.

Don't be afraid to get parents involved in this. The same principles that apply to students apply to your parents. Get them involved, and your job just keeps getting easier and easier, allowing you the time you need to do what you really need to do—teach. If you can get your parents on board and get them to take ownership in the organization, you have definitely come a long way in developing your leadership abilities.

Creating Ownership in the Group

How do you gain ownership in a company? Typically, you "buy in" by purchasing stock or sharing ownership with other shareholders. By purchasing stock in a company, you expect to get returns on your investment. You go into this knowing there are risks involved. When you get a return on your investment, you are likely to invest even more in the company.

It is the same with a large group effort. If you can get your students to buy into your program, they will have a greater appreciation for the direction the group is heading. There must be an expected gain on the part of the students. As co-owners with you in the organization, they will also expect to share in the decisions. If you utilize them in too small a way, they are likely to ask for more. If you can get your students to this point, it becomes an enriching experience for all involved.

This is where student leadership can play a critical role in your organization. Developing student leaders will help the student develop skills that are impossible to teach through simply lecturing or propping yourself up as dictator. As an added benefit, student leaders can also do many of the busywork tasks that can bog down an active leader.

The thoroughness and professionalism of a well-motivated student leader constantly amazes me. The embarrassing fact is that they sometimes do a better job than I would have done myself. I have one such student leader in my high school band who has made my life incredibly easy over the last four years.

His name is Tyler, and he has an amazingly energetic and charismatic persona. When you consider Maslow and his Hierarchy of Needs, Tyler is the perfect example of transcendence. He seeks the betterment of others and is just the type of leader I have described in this book.

In four short years, he has been my music librarian, announcer at concerts and contests, narrator for several productions, drum major, attendance taker, advisor, student conductor, and trusted friend. I consider him my unpaid assistant director. He has done this for free and without complaint. He has accomplished tasks for me that I never asked him to do and frankly never even knew needed to be done. He is a senior this year, and I don't know how I will get along without him. You can inspire this sort of student leadership when you find ways to get students to buy into your program.

Taking ownership in a group allows the student to lead the group in small ways and therefore gives them a stake in the success of the group along with a sense of shared responsibility when the group fails to succeed. By allowing a student into your leadership world, you share something with the student that he or she may never get anywhere else. Student leadership then becomes infectious throughout the entire group and becomes the "in thing" to do. Other non-motivated students become energized to show their own leadership within your program, and eventually, the entire group will jump on board making your job much easier or irrelevant. If you can move students to this point, sit back, sip some tea, and enjoy the cool breeze given off by all the busy bodies around you.

Feedback
Don't ignore the core. Your group as a whole will have an opinion. You need to realize that you may not always see the entire picture. Seeking feedback from your group will tell them that you care. Remember the cliché, "Students do not care what you know until they know that you care." Seeking feedback, adjusting strategies based on feedback, and giving credit to the core of your group will ensure that the large group you lead will buy into what they are doing and take ownership of their program.

Making yourself available to your students is not always convenient. I know of some teachers who will not publish their phone numbers and turn off their cell phones on the weekend. Although I do understand why they do this, making yourself unapproachable is not something that enhances credibility as a leader.

A successful leader will answer emails in a timely manner and get back to people when they need something. Being available to your students is necessary, but there do need to be some boundaries. Make sure they know what your boundaries are, and then make yourself available in ways that fit your style and wishes.

Personally, I encourage my students to send me emails or text messages. I publish my cell phone number and email address for all the students. That way, I can answer their questions on my own terms and time. This also provides me a way to answer in a more intelligent manner.

I have found that much of my need to answer feedback and questions comes from a lack of good communication. When I explain concepts in class thoroughly and send out schedules with detailed information in emails, I answer fewer questions along the way. This saves me time and trouble and makes everyone's job easier.

One further consideration is this: Keep your communications to students, especially written communications, brief and professional. Resist the urge to joke around, and keep everything you say appropriate. If a student sends you anything that is inappropriate, do not answer. Forward the communication to your principal, and avoid having anything to do with a communication that might get you fired.

Praise and Adoration
The other side of feedback is praise. Praise is the feedback you give your students when they go beyond expectations. To be an effective charismatic leader, you must learn to control praise. Giving praise liberally is a mistake. There is great value in praise, but true praise is earned and not merely given out at random. There are certain situations where praise is not appropriate, and if you abuse this power, you will lose your impact as an effective leader.

Praise should not be offered to students for doing ordinary jobs that you expect as part of their normal responsibilities. Giving too much praise for small tasks will minimize the impact of your praise when excellence is observed. Being overly generous with your praise can come across as condescending or fake.

Additionally, praise should not be offered when a student stops a poor behavior. Good behavior is an expectation. Giving praise for behaving only satisfies the desire for acceptance. Many times, students misbehave to gain attention, and when you praise them for stopping, you are asking for a repeat performance from that student. Instead, give praise to the well-behaved students around the troublemaker. When you wag this bone in front of the misbehaving students, you can guarantee they will earn your praise the right way.

Have you ever noticed how your love life goes when it comes to affection? When you truly liked someone, you most likely showed too much affection and drove the person away. When you didn't care for a person as much, you showed much less affection. Have you ever noticed that the person to whom you showed less affection was the one you couldn't get rid of?

This is what happens when you create a shortage of a desired emotion. By withholding this emotion, you create a wanting in the other person. A shortage always creates demand. This works amazingly well with praise.

If you withhold praise, you will create a shortage. Students will desire your praise and go above and beyond to get your approval, especially if they respect your opinions and value your leadership. When you finally do praise their extraordinary efforts, chances are they will soak it up like a sponge.

You can also create this desire by overly praising one deserving student in front of the entire class. I don't know about you, but when I see someone get a gift, I want one as well. Coveting another person's success is a normal function of a healthy mind. By encouraging one student, you raise the value of your praise and create a higher demand for your adoration.

There are other unique ways to use praise to motivate students. The next time you notice students repeating a poor behavior, praise them for the opposite of what you observe. In other words, praise them for doing what you want them to do instead of telling them what they are doing wrong.

I have used this many times in my band classes. When I hear students giving a dull performance, I praise them for their incredible sound. I then tell them how impressed I am by their energy and ask for even more. The students suddenly feel like they have my approval, and this creates what I was originally wanting. If I had approached the problem by telling them how sorry they sounded, I would have completely turned them the other direction. Be wise in how you use this tactic. If you are too obvious, your students will see right through you.

I have also noticed an interesting side effect of approval and praise. Over the last eighteen years, I have raised hundreds of thousands of dollars in fundraising. I have observed that it is a statistical certainty that some of my least musically successful students will be my best sellers. It took me some time to figure out why, but I eventually stumbled on the answer.

These students were aware of their failure in my class and noticed my lack of praise. Fundraising turned out to be an easy task that they could successfully accomplish. In return, they received my praise in the form of public recognition and prizes. I had one trumpet player who was dead last in his section but sold $1,500 worth of cookie dough in two weeks of selling. It took him the next three weeks to make his deliveries. The band boosters had to purchase a freezer to keep his products frozen while he did his work. This clearly demonstrates the power of withholding praise.

Although this is a powerful example, this idea of withholding praise should not be used to exploit your students for profit. I have never encouraged my less motivated students to gain my approval through fundraising. This is merely a recurring phenomenon. I assume that this occurs frequently, and there are many other examples that could be used. The bottom line is this: Use your praise wisely, and don't be too liberal if you want praise to be effective.

¼ Teaspoon of Disappointment
Praise is powerful, but disappointment is mighty! Put them together, and you get a mighty powerful ingredient for your educational soup. If you choose to mix these two ingredients into the pot, be careful not to mix in too much disappointment, or you'll spoil the soup. This ingredient can make the eyes water, so sprinkle on lightly. Disappointment can enhance the flavor of praise and makes your soup come alive.

Selling Your Success and Spreading the Good News
If you can manage to bring your group to success, you need to spread the good news through as many outlets as possible. This is the kind of praise that you need to dish out with multiple servings. As a group leader, you have the responsibility to contact newspapers, send out congratulatory emails, or do anything else that will let people know what you have accomplished. You can't win if you don't enter, so get the word out there.

When you send out a general congratulatory e-mail, don't just send it to your own building. Remember that several of the teachers in the other schools have had these students and will be eager to see their accomplishments. Not only does this put a feather in your cap, but now the other teachers know who you are and that you are doing a good job with their former students. Your success becomes theirs.

Spreading the news about success also enhances your chances of gaining support from your administration. If your administration is like mine, they are too busy to keep up with every detail of your program. Too often, they must focus their attention on the negative aspects of the school district. You need to draw their attention to you so they can see something positive for a change. It is good to be associated with the overall success of the school district. This is, after all, what your administrators are working so hard to help you accomplish.

Support generally flows toward success, so point the stream your way. There is nothing better for your self-esteem than knowing your boss thinks you are great. The next time you need to order textbooks or buy a new tuba, drawing on the memory of past success will help your cause and give your administrators confidence in your abilities and decisions.

You need to do whatever it takes to build positive perception about your activity or program. Find anything that even remotely looks like success and get it out to the public. Simply saying thank you to someone or sending out an email telling people how much you appreciate their help with a recent contest is as good as advertising in the newspaper. Make your success their success. Anything your students do that is successful needs to be seen by as many people as possible.

A web page can be the ultimate broadcasting tool for success. Not only can people see what is happening in your program, but they can also see what has been happening. This type of exposure is an effective way to enhance community perception. Success breeds success, and being able to advertise your accomplishments can only enhance this process.

Are there businesses in town owned by your supporters? How about taking a picture of your students with their new trophy and framing it for the restaurants' walls? Business owners love to show off their kids' accomplishments. There is no better place to hang the picture. You may eventually find an entire section of the business devoted to your program.

Check out the magazines in your educational area. They are likely looking for submissions or story ideas. If you have something worth sharing, contact a magazine, and get your work in front of a larger audience.

A few years ago, this idea worked very well for me. I had built a recording studio for my music technology class, and a bevy of powerful audio equipment surrounded us in our newly constructed auditorium. I was also using our distance-learning lab as a way to bring clinicians to our campus. The spring concert was also approaching, and we were planning a multimedia performance with the theater screen above the stage.

I was browsing a band magazine one day and noticed that they wanted submissions for their upcoming technology issue. I outlined my use of technology in an email and found myself on the cover the next month. The headline on the cover said, "Stephen McClard, A Natural Progression to Music Technology." I was very proud of that moment, and the cover hanging on my wall reminds me of that every day. My administrators were not aware of my innovative ideas, and when the magazine arrived on the superintendent's desk one day, he made sure the entire community knew.

A few years later, the same magazine sent out a personal request for my educational biography. They had noticed the successes on our band web page and connected me with the earlier magazine article. I submitted my biography and became one of their "50 Band Directors Who Make a Difference." I was the only band director from Missouri in that issue, and the pride and honor I felt made me know that I was appreciated for my work.

Our band program has been listed as one of the "Top 100 Best Schools for Music Education in America" four times as voted by several educational organizations around the country. We received this honor because of our dedication to music education and because we filled out the survey. It is important to deserve the honor, and you must do what you can to spread the news. One small action on your part can make all the difference.

Selling apparel is another way to identify your program as successful. We decided a few years ago that we would produce a hoodie for our eighth-grade band to wear to a football game. We have them perform once a year with the high school band at a home game, and we decided along the way to offer the apparel to anyone who wanted to order. We further decided to offer several options like sweatshirts, t-shirts, and long-sleeve tees. When we placed the order, we had $4,500 worth of merchandise sold. Since that time, we have done this with great success each year. I can't go anywhere in our town without seeing our logo going down the street. Branding and advertising can have an amazing impact on your program and identifies your students with their group. Do not underestimate the pride this instills.

I have one caution when selling the success of your team. Be careful not to come across as a braggart. It is very easy to make your success a thorn in the side of a less fortunate program or teacher. Misery loves company, and when you are the wrong company, misery will be your worst nightmare. To avoid this, be proud, but also be humble when selling your success. Recognize the success of others and focus on the students instead of yourself.

Understanding the Difference Between Manipulation and Lies
Building a team is difficult when faced with untruthfulness and manipulation. Students are experimenting with behavior at this point in their lives, and it is important that we help them develop in the proper way. Being able to tell the difference between truth and lies is important to building a team. Being able to push students to be better people will require your gentle willingness to help them see the error in their ways. Do not damage self-esteem in the process.

Teenagers are famous for asking manipulative questions when they want something. They are actually very good at it. Lies can be hidden in questions and comments, so it is necessary for a group leader to know how to handle this problem.

It is usually not very hard to tell if a student is lying. The hard part is making them admit to the lie without having them lose face. Most lies are innocent ways of hiding the fear of rejection or disagreement from the teacher. With practice, you can become a walking lie detector and possess the capacity to handle the problem without harming the child's self-concept.

To determine if someone is being manipulative or untruthful, check the body language given off. First, look for a stiff physical expression. A person who is manipulative or lying will most often make body movements in an inward way as if hiding something. They will avoid eye contact. Some sources would have you believe that the direction of eye movement will tell you for sure that someone is lying. This has more to do with self-esteem than lying and is not an accurate way of checking for truthfulness. This is especially true in girls. Despite this fact, eye movement can be helpful in determining truthfulness but should not be your only indication.

One of the best ways that I have found to deal with this problem is not to say a word after a student asks a manipulative question. I pause for a few seconds and look into the student's eyes. This throws him off so badly that he instantly wonders how you know he is lying. Even if you only suspect a lie, this method is nearly foolproof. If the student is being truthful, he will simply ask you why you are looking at him so weird. If he is lying, he will stumble all over himself with further embellishment. Watch the eyes. As you look at him, he will typically look away if he is lying.

This also works very well if you suspect manipulation. If a student tells you, for instance, that she will be unable to attend an after-school tutoring session, she will probably follow it up with, "Is that okay with you?" If you answer her or ask more questions, she will probably keep manipulating you. If you stand there, looking at her without saying a word, she will immediately go into panic mode if she is manipulating you. If you stand there long enough, she will eventually come up with the best answer and just give up. If she is being honest, then she will just ask why you are acting so weird.

There are certain indications that give the manipulator away. The appeal will always be to move you from common sense to emotion. There is a certain feeling you get inside when someone speaks to you and your heart says, "Wait, that's not right." When you feel this inner conflict (instant cognitive dissonance), then be warned that you are probably being manipulated. An appeal to ego, guilt, intimidation, fear, curiosity, or desire to be liked should be a dead giveaway that you should remain logical and keep your ground. Your ability to mediate your thinking will keep you driving to the correct decision.

Remember what your rules and policies are, and be consistent. A manipulator will try to get you to bend your policies, so be on guard. Help them see that being truthful is the best way to show their leadership to you and the group.

This chapter sure was packed with useful information that any teachers in their right minds would love to give out as advice. Consider giving this book as a gift to a friend, student teacher, co-worker, or family member. You might even want to slip a copy under the last roll of toilet paper in the teacher's bathroom. Donations are tax deductible, so give liberally.

34
Dealing with Willful Misbehavior

"Eighteen years of teaching have taught me one very clear lesson. Experience and emotion drives all behavior, good or bad. Because of this, I can only control a certain percentage of circumstances based on my own experiences. These circumstances are further restricted by my abilities and emotional control as a leader. If I can somehow enhance my experiences and exert greater ability and emotional control, I can, in turn, control more of my environment." Quoted from Chapter 2

I saved this chapter for last because dealing with willful misbehavior is the last action you will take. After trying everything that you have read so far, dealing with extreme misbehavior and disruptive attitudes may require tough choices. What you have learned above may help you avoid the need to dish out punishment. Despite this, punishment will be inevitable. The following may help you decide how you will proceed.

Pause a moment and consider the larger picture.
Wouldn't it be nice if all students came from structured families and attended amazing churches? Wouldn't it be great if students received constant stimulation at home and parents met every need? To be honest, I don't think that is the way God intended it to be. We learn from failure, and God probably knows this better than anyone does. If the world were perfect, how would we ever recognize success, and how would we know what good actually means? Be thankful for the misbehaving student. They make you realize just how special the students are who have the will to behave. Finding ways to move all students to willfully behave well is therefore your entire job.

You will no doubt experience a broad spectrum of behavior in your classroom. All your skills to this point may be ineffective in the shadow of willful misbehavior. There are those few students who are constant repeat offenders with no apparent conscience. Think about what I said earlier. It takes an unbalanced force to move an object from its equilibrium. This is true unless you are a feather moving a bowling ball. It may not happen unless you can get someone who knows how to bowl to help you out. Don't be afraid to seek help, and don't seek help because you lack the drive to do it yourself.

The key, then, is getting the right help. In this case, the parent should be your first alternative. A parent can be an effective help with a willful child or no help at all. The parent, after all, may be the real problem, so it is critical for you to find this out first.

Several of my past students would regularly show up without reeds. When I met the parents, saw a pack of cigarettes in their top pocket, and smelled liquor on their breath, it suddenly became clear why the student could not afford the proper equipment. Sometimes you need to use common sense when dealing with these matters and determine where the problem really originates. Is continually showing up without reeds a discipline issue or a need? Are the parents working for the child or against the child?

I can remember yelling at a student for missing a concert. His absence was very upsetting. I found out that his mother was regularly drunk and had never attended any of our performances. The student attended past concerts, and it later dawned on me that it had rained on the night of this particular concert. He walked to the other concerts and could not that evening because of the rain. The next performance came, and I gave him a ride. As I recall, we even grabbed some fast food on the way. What made the difference here? Was it the yelling or the compassion that I showed the student?

The next stop might be the principal. A good principal is trained to deal with harsh behavior and has a clear process to help you deal with this sort of child. It is entirely possible that a few days in ISS will solve your problem. Then again, it may not. If your principal or school district is ineffective, you may be on your own.

No matter what you try, make sure you document your efforts. All students should be afforded due process. Document each technique that you try and share this with your principal and the parents of the student in question.

As you find out more about the situations, always ask yourself if there is anything you are doing as a teacher that may have contributed to the problem. Try a new approach if this is the case. Sometimes this constant effort on your part is all it takes to let everyone involved know that you care enough for them to make a change. It helps if you have great charisma and a high degree of respect in the community. Students respect the fact that someone wants to help make them better, so make sure you first appeal to this emotional need.

One person you should not discount in helping you with a discipline issue is your school counselor. The school guidance counselor can deal with certain emotional issues that you may be incapable of perceiving or managing. Some extreme problems that you have in the classroom are simply reactions to situations outside the classroom. The school counselor may be just the person to give this student the attention that he needs to climb over the problem.

If all else fails, you will face the truth. The truth has been around for a long time, and we all must succumb to its power and constancy. You reap what you sow. There is no escaping this truth.

There are so many problems in our lives that create cross roads: the death of a parent, the abuse of a relative, health problems of family members, and the list goes on. You can only do so much to guide young minds, and the rest is up to the choices they make. They will learn this lesson of reaping and sowing, and sometimes you need to push them in another direction to make them realize this truth.

If that bowling ball starts rolling down a hill toward a cliff, there will be little anyone can do to stop it once it gains momentum. Your best efforts as an educator, even the greatest of educators, are of little significance when a student, for whatever reason, rejects the pursuit of knowledge and the betterment of his future. After all options are exhausted, you may need to make tough choices. Removing a student from your class, school, or activity may be your only choice.

As a band director and large-group instructor, I face this dilemma often. I have concluded that it is better to drop a student from band than keep him in the activity where he can harm the other students who want to succeed. After making every attempt, teaching the student the lesson of reaping and sowing may be the best and last lesson he will learn from me as an educator.

If removing a defiant student from an activity or school altogether teaches him the lesson of consequences, then my job as an educator may be successful after all. You never know, learning this life lesson may save him from losing a job later on in life or from ending up in prison. Drawing on our past successes or failures will drive our decisions no matter who we are.

Concluding Thoughts

"You cannot open a book without learning something." Confucius, 500 B.C.

I have thoroughly enjoyed writing this book. Writing these thoughts down has motivated and inspired me. After reading my own words, I now realize that I need to get busy and practice what I have preached. These words reveal my own weaknesses as an educator and give me a renewed enthusiasm for the next fifteen years.

I hope that this book will help you become the teacher that you set out to be. Having reflected on your own personal leadership style, I hope that I have inspired you to come up with your own specialized tools and educational routines. This may allow you to experience your job in a more meaningful and fulfilling way.

Whatever you do, do not use all the techniques in this book in one day. You will drive yourself crazy, and your students will think you are on drugs. Take one technique at a time, and make it work for you. Add one tool to your belt at a time, and keep it sharp. Once you have accomplished this, continue to improve your knowledge in the area you teach. Having amazing leadership skills will be of no value without good content.

If you take nothing else from this book, remember that to succeed as an educator or large-group leader only takes optimism in your abilities and confidence in your skills. Never stop developing your skills and never be afraid to take charge. Move yourself forward in a calm and assertive manner and move your students in meaningful and positive ways. In doing this, you and your students can realize the full potential that this world offers to those who choose to succeed. In the end, you will see previous problems melt away and eventually turn failure into success. The "one" that can make the difference is you.

Classroom Questions and Activities

1. Reflect on how the concepts found in this book will help you become a superior educator. Share your story at www.superiored.com.

Recommended Resources

The following books and resources were valuable in the writing of this book. These resources may provide further insight to the topics covered.

Curwin, Richard and Allen Mendler. *Discipline with Dignity*. Association for Supervision & Curriculum Development; 2nd edition (September 1999).

Dreikurs, Rudolf. *Fundamentals of Adlerian Psychology*. Adler School of Professional (June 1975).

Gladwell, Malcolm. *Blink*. Back Bay Books (2007).

Jacobsen, Rowan. *Chocolate Unwrapped*. Invisible Cities Press Llc; illustrated edition (2003).

Legee, James. *Chinese Classics Series*. Simon Publications (August 2001).

Maslow, Abraham. *A Theory of Human Motivation*. Originally Published in *Psychological Review*, 50, 370-396 (1943).

O'Sullivan, Mary. *Why Sleep?* Quanta Dynamics (2003).

About the Author
Stephen T. McClard

Stephen T. McClard has been the Director of Bands at Bolivar High School since 2002. Mr. McClard graduated from Southeast Missouri State University in 1990. He started his teaching career in Southeast Missouri before moving to Illinois where he taught band for 8 years.

Mr. McClard's bands have consistently received superior ratings at contest as well as many other awards and accolades. Since 2002, the band has traveled twice to Chicago, where they won 1st place class 4A and 1st place overall at the Midwest Music in the Parks Festival. The band also traveled to Cincinnati in 2006, receiving the same honors.

In 2006, Mr. McClard was named by SBO Magazine as one of the 50 Directors Who Make a Difference. In 2006, 2008, and 2009, Bolivar R-I School district was named one of the "Best 100 Communities for Music Education" in America by the American Music Conference. Mr. McClard was previously featured on the cover of the 2003 issue of *School Band and Orchestra Magazine* for his work with music technology.

In addition to his career in education, Mr. McClard maintains an online woodworking business and is a third-generation piano technician. His woodworking creations include custom bass guitars, which have sold all over the world and one-of-a-kind computer desks made from old pianos. His piano desks have been featured in magazines such as *Business 2.0* and *Piano Technicians Journal* and in many other newspapers and television news features.